Victorian Panorama

NEWCASTLE-UPON-TYNE IN THE REIGN OF QUEEN VICTORIA.

'I know not where to seek, even in this busy country, a spot or district in which we perceive so extraordinary and multifarious a combination of the various great branches of mining, manufacturing, trading, and shipbuilding industry, and I greatly doubt whether the like can be shown, not only within the limits of this land but upon the whole surface of the globe.'

Extract from the speech of the Right Hon. W.E. Gladstone, Chancellor of the Exchequer, on his visit to Newcastle upon Tyne, 1862.

Victorian Panorama

A visit to Newcastle upon Tyne in the Reign of Queen Victoria

Alan Morgan

Tyne Bridge Publishing

Acknowledgements

The author would like to thank local historians Stan Cairns, Richard E. Keys, R.W. Rennison, and Anthea Lang of Gateshead Local Studies, for help and advice in the preparation of this book. He would also like to thank the staff of Newcastle Libraries Local Studies for their enthusiastic assistance.

Tyne Bridge Publishing thank printers Elanders Hindson Ltd for their generous support of this book. Thanks also to Marie-Therese Mayne of the Laing Art Gallery, Tyne & Wear Museums, for her help.

Designed by Anna Flowers, Tyne Bridge Publishing.

Illustrations are from the collections of and ©Newcastle Libraries unless otherwise indicated.

The enlarged details of John Storey's sepia lithograph, *Newcastle upon Tyne in the Reign of Queen Victoria* are reproduced from a copy belonging to Newcastle Libraries.

ISBN 978 195795 104 2

Published by City of Newcastle upon Tyne
Newcastle Libraries & Information Service,
Tyne Bridge Publishing, 2007

www.tynebridgepublishing.co.uk

Printed by Elanders Hindson, North Tyneside

Front cover: coloured lithograph *Newcastle upon Tyne in the Reign of Queen Victoria* by John Storey, 1862
©Laing Art Gallery, Tyne & Wear Museums.

Also by Alan Morgan
A Fine and Private Place: Jesmond Old Cemetery
Beyond the Grave: Exploring Newcastle's Burial Grounds

Contents

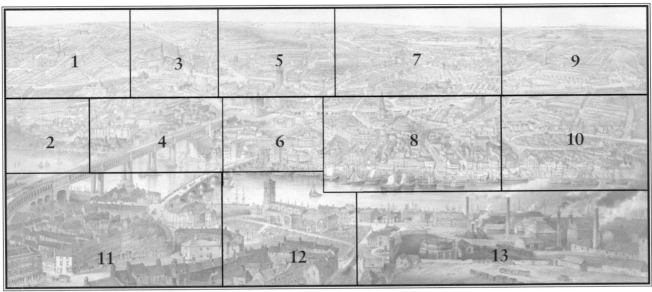

Key to John Storey's Newcastle upon Tyne in the Reign of Queen Victoria.

Entries within each chapter are headed in red if the street or structure has been demolished, or in blue if they can still be seen.

John Storey 1827-1888, artist

John Storey was born in Newcastle upon Tyne on 23 October 1827, the second of nine children. The son of a schoolmaster, he was educated at his father's 'classical and commercial boarding school' at Picton Place, and later St Mary's Place. There were over 110 academies for boys and girls in mid-Victorian Newcastle, some of which took boarders.

He must have shown an early talent for art as he was then taken as a pupil by Thomas Miles Richardson senior, 'that great master of water colour painting'.

In 1844 John made a drawing of the opening of Gateshead's railway station. It was praised as 'a faithful representation of the building which reflects great credit on the ability of the young artist who is not yet 18.'

However, several years later, perhaps at a time when he was seeking to establish himself as an artist, he is described variously as a commission agent, a merchant, a shipbroker, a coal exporter, and a corn merchant.

Without doubt John Storey's most impressive works are the two watercolours *Newcastle upon Tyne in the Reign of Queen Elizabeth* (1854), and *Newcastle upon Tyne in the Reign of Queen Victoria* (1862) (and the lithograph based upon it), which is explored in this book.

One of John Storey's particular talents was perspective drawing and he worked closely with the local authorities on

The Laing Art Gallery, Tyne & Wear Museums

Newcastle upon Tyne in the Reign of Queen Elizabeth by John Storey (watercolour).

A view of Wallsend illustrating J. Collingwood Bruce's 'Account of the Roman Wall', 1851. Drawn and engraved by John Storey.

The Laing Art Gallery, Tyne & Wear Museums

King Street, near the Black Gate, 1882 (watercolour).

public works, and with some of Newcastle's leading architects, making drawings of important projects.

He was also commissioned to draw and engrave some of the illustrations for Dr John Collingwood Bruce's *Account of the Roman Wall* of 1851. After a day's sketching near the Wall he would relax in the evening at The Chesters, the Northumberland home of Town Clerk and antiquarian John Clayton, amusing fellow guests with his good natured humour.

Ecclesiastical buildings were another favourite subject and included York Minster, Whitby Abbey, Durham Cathedral, Tynemouth Priory and St Nicholas' Church. He had many professional engagements all over the North of England.

Storey's final paintings, specifically for the Royal Jubilee Exhibition of 1887, were *The Heart of Newcastle from the South*, and *A View of Castle Garth*.

Storey married late in life and lived in fashionable

Lovaine Place. After a spell of illness in the 1880s he moved to Harrogate in the hope that his health would improve. He died there, aged 60, on 9 March 1888, and is buried in Westgate Hill Cemetery. He was one of the last of the school of Newcastle painters represented by the Richardsons, Henry Perlee Parker, and J.W. Carmichael.

The watercolour *Newcastle upon Tyne in the Reign of Queen Victoria*, and the lithograph based upon it, takes a bird's eye view of Newcastle, and part of Gateshead, from an imaginary vantage point above Gateshead's former railway station, Brandling Junction. Artistic licence has been employed to emphasise certain structures, either by size or a marginal shift in position. The painting bears the date 1862; the two editions of the print are dated 1862 and 1864 and feature a quotation from the speech made by W.E. Gladstone on his visit to Newcastle as Chancellor of the Exchequer on 7 October 1862.

NOW ON VIEW,
MR. JOHN STOREY'S very beautiful and elaborate Drawing of
NEWCASTLE-UPON-TYNE IN THE REIGN OF QUEEN VICTORIA, 1862,
Forming the long-promised Companion to his popular Picture of
NEWCASTLE-UPON-TYNE IN THE REIGN OF QUEEN ELIZABETH, 1562.
Prices, to Subscribers, from One to Two Guineas each.
AT R. TURNER'S FINE ARTS GALLERY,
32, GREY STREET, NEWCASTLE.UPON-TYNE.
N.B.—Admission Free.   No Invitation Cards issued.

Newcastle Daily Journal, Tuesday 25 November 1862.

Visitors were invited to view the 'very beautiful and elaborate Drawing of Newcastle upon Tyne in the Reign of Queen Victoria, 1862', at R. Turner's Fine Arts Gallery at 32 Grey Street from 25th November, 1862. Prints were on sale to subscribers from one to two guineas each (presumably depending upon size).

Newcastle Daily Chronicle featured a lengthy and very favourable review of the picture two days later on Thursday 27 November. The reviewer tells us that Storey had been commissioned to paint it ten years earlier (when he would

have been only 25 years old) and that the delay in completion was because he was waiting for the fire damage on the Quayside to be replaced with new buildings. He goes on to describe Storey's most important picture.

> The perspective is charmingly managed, conveying the impression of space and distance most completely. The scene is bright and refreshing, bathed in sunshine, except here and there, where some passing cloud casts a passing shadow … the colouring is warm and harmonious, but not too glowing for this northern latitude. We are sure that very few of the numerous persons who throng its busy streets had an adequate idea that "Canny Newcastle" possessed so many elements of the picturesque as Mr Storey has successfully shown it to contain.
>
> … On casting the eye over the town the magnitude of the splendid architectural achievements with which the genius of Grainger adorned its streets is at once seen by the most casual observer. A more careful examination of the details reveals the fact that the painting of the innumerable public and private buildings has been painstaking and surprisingly correct, the most minute details being depicted … all the more prominent objects are perfect miniatures of the originals.
>
> … A striking object in the foreground is St Mary's Church, Gateshead, beautifully drawn; and on the banks of the river to the east are the works of Messrs Abbott, the mingled clouds of steam and dark smoke towering above them being indicative of the operations going on actively beneath. The site of Gateshead's new quay and the locality of the ever-memorable explosion … a view of Bottle Bank and the streets running towards Tyne Bridge, crowded with vehicles and passengers.

… It is impossible to give in detail the whole of its numerous beauties; and to be justly appreciated an inspection of the picture itself is necessary. We would urge those of our readers who have not already done so, not to lose the opportunity of seeing for themselves a picture which is at once a surprising work of art and a monument of the greatness of the town. We may state that the talented artist is a native of Newcastle.

Some of the structures shown in the picture were not built until after 1862, so unless Storey possessed second sight we must conclude that he had access to architects' plans and was attempting to make his picture of Newcastle as up to date and as forward looking as possible. They include the Tyne Brewery (1868), St John's Angus Works (1868), the Royal Grammar School (1870), the spire of St Mary's Cathedral (1872), and the Tyne Tees Shipping office (1875). These buildings were all planned long before they were finally completed. The intention of the picture is very much to convey the progress, industry and prosperity of the town, which 20 years later would become a city.

The watercolour *Newcastle upon Tyne in the Reign of Queen Victoria* is in the collections of the Laing Art Gallery, Newcastle upon Tyne.

These verses by James Horsley are quoted in an obituary of John Storey, 1888. 'T.B.' refers to Thomas Bewick.

D'yee knaa John Storey? Yes, aa ken him weel;
A clivvor chap, besides a sonsie chiel;
A gentleman, and yet sae kind and free,
He'll crack a joke wiv either ye or me.

Div aa ken John Storey? Man yor question's odd;
Div aa kna St Nicklas? says wor frind John Todd;

Aa ken him, an' aa've knaan him frev a pup.
Not knaa John Storey? Wey, aa browt him up!

There's not a pictor in ma hoose ye'll see
That's not John Storey's, except one–T.B.
Didn't Richardson declare, his oath upon,
That only two could paint–hissel and John.

Thor's not a bonny place nigh hand wor Tyne
But he's painted till it leuks divine;
His Aad and New Newcassel, leuk at them;
Not knaa John Storey? Man, ye should think sheym!
Tom Richardson's greet pupil; wey, ye clod,
Better say ye divvent knaa John Todd!

Alan Morgan

The Storey family plot in Westgate Cemetery. It has been damaged over the years. John Storey, his grandmother, parents, and five of his brothers and sisters are buried here.

John Storey's Newcastle – a few facts

Newcastle's vital statistics

A population of 109,108 in 1861 (33,048 in 1801).

A circumference of 16 miles and an area of 5,325 acres.

632 streets.

13,000 dwellings.

2,170 public lights.

23 postmen and 16 clerks, based at the Royal Arcade.

Three daily, five weekly, newspapers.

Police and fire

140 police officers in Newcastle based at Manors, Westgate, Percy Street and Ouseburn. Uniforms were blue (deposit of £4 required).

33 police officers in Gateshead.

20 river policemen, including four officers, with six rowing boats available.

2 fire stations in Newcastle financed by fire insurance companies, plus several private brigades. A town fire brigade was formed in 1867.

Gateshead established a volunteer fire brigade in 1857 with 33 men, all policemen, and a second-hand fire engine, axes, buckets, leather helmets and 650ft of leather hose.

Major employers

The coal industry created jobs in mines and all aspects of export and distribution.

Other employers included engineering works, iron foundries, rope makers, chain cable and anchor smiths, shipyards, bottle and glassworks, earthenware factories, brickyards, chemical works (including alkali, copperas, and soda), coachbuilding (about 1000 coaches manufactured annually).

Some smaller employers listed in J. Collingwood Bruce's *Handbook* to Newcastle for 1863 are papermaking, tanneries, tobacco manufacturers, flax mills, flour mills, clay pipe makers, white and red lead manufacturers.

Local coach travel

You could travel by coach to many local destinations:

Chester-le-Street, Durham and Leadgate – daily from the Wheatsheaf Inn, Cloth Market.

Blaydon – three times a day from the Alnwick House Inn, Cloth Market.

Otterburn – daily from the Garrick's Head Inn, Cloth Market.

Matfen, Stamfordham and Whittingham – every Tuesday and Saturday from the Victoria Hotel, Newgate Street.

Belsay – Tuesdays, Thursdays and Saturdays from the Phoenix Inn, Newgate Street.

Dirty old town

In the 1850s Lord Palmerston commented that 'Newcastle's inhabitants would rather see their neighbours perish around them and risk the lives of their wives and children and their own, rather than ward off the dangers by arrangements which might involve a sixpenny rate.'

Thanks to Newcastle's entrepreneurs, industry was booming and people were flooding into town to find work. Overcrowding was the result. In poorer areas of town many families lived in one-room dwellings, with no piped water or sanitary facilities. In the Sandgate area 5,000 were crowded into 350 houses with four private WCs, one public privy and three private privies. In the town as a whole there were only 1,421 WCs.

There was an appalling build up of dung (human and animal) in the lanes and alleys of the town. It was collected into six main depots and some was used as fertiliser on the Town Moor, but this led to further problems as the Moor was the source of some of Newcastle's water supply.

Smoke from industrial and domestic chimneys, and other

Dwellings in the Groat Market, 1855.

noxious fumes, meant air quality was very poor.

Newcastle's mortality rate was about 282 per thousand, higher than in any other provincial town except Liverpool and Manchester.

Not all housing was substandard. There was much new building as better-off people moved away from the riverside and out to the suburbs. Conditions were much more pleasant for the middle classes. For example in Richard Grainger's town centre housing developments there were 414 households (including 517 WCs) for 2,070 people. This didn't mean they were immune to the deadly cholera; 28 people died in Grainger's streets in 1853.

The 1853 cholera epidemic affected all parts of town, not just poorer parts, because some of the water piped into town came from the Tyne at Elswick.

A Newcastle timeline 1852-1865

1852   Launch of the *John Bowes*, first screw-propelled iron collier, start of serious shipbuilding on Tyne.

1853   Medical School moves to Orchard Street.

1853   Cholera epidemic. 1,533 perish in Newcastle.

1854   Great fire at Gateshead spreads to Newcastle.

1854   Birth of Charles Parsons, inventor of steam turbine.

1855   W.G. Armstrong invents breech-loading gun.

1857   Northumberland Dock opens at Howdon.

1858   Work begins on reconstruction of Quayside.

1859   Death of Robert Stephenson, age 56.

1859   W.G. Armstrong knighted.

1860   Dr J.H. Rutherford becomes pastor at Bath Lane Congregational Church.

1860   Robert Stephenson Works biggest local employer.

1861   Death of Richard Grainger, age 63.

1862   George Stephenson Monument unveiled.

1862   *Blaydon Races* song first sung by Geordie Ridley.

1863   Last public execution in Newcastle.

1863   Portico added to Central Station.

1863   Robert Chambers wins World Sculling Championships.

1864   Railway opens between Newcastle and the Coast.

1865   Death of John Dobson, age 77.

A window on the wider world 1852-1865

1852   Death of Duke of Wellington, age 83.

1853   Queen Victoria given chloroform during labour.

1854   E.G. Otis invents hydraulic lift.

1854   Crimean War begins, ends 1856.

1855   Celluloid invented.

1856   Thomas Cook's first travel tour to Europe.

1856   Queen Victoria institutes Victoria Cross.

1857   Louis Pasteur discovers pasteurisation of milk.

1858   First Atlantic cable laid.

1859   Charles Dickens, *A Tale of Two Cities*.

1859   Pullman luxury railway coaches invented.

1859   Charles Darwin, *The Origin of Species*.

1861   Mrs Beeton, *Book of Household Management*.

1861   Prince Albert dies of typhoid, age 42.

1861   American Civil War begins; ends 1865.

1863   Football Association founded.

1863   World's first underground railway opens in London.

1863   Co-operative Wholesale Society established.

1864   Red Cross founded.

1865   Salvation Army founded.

1865   Discovery of antiseptic surgery by Joseph Lister.

Local pride – the unveiling of the Monument to George Stephenson, 2 October, 1862. The day was a holiday and cheap excursion trains brought thousands to town. Local engineering workers, with banners, and local militia regiments paraded through the streets. Just three weeks later John Storey's panorama of Newcastle, which features the monument, would go on show at R. Turner's Fine Arts Gallery on Grey Street.

1 Arthur's Hill to the Infirmary

1 Westgate Hill Cemetery

Newcastle's first private cemetery opened in 1829 to provide an alternative to the town's overcrowded burial grounds. It was primarily for non-conformists. The cemetery was never consecrated and the last burial took place about 1961. John Storey was buried here in 1888.

2 Elswick Quarry (red entries indicate a vanished place)

Isaac Cookson, the industrialist, owned the quarry which provided stone for, among other purposes, local Victorian housing. The area is now covered by modern housing with some open spaces.

3 Arthur's Hill

Initially consisted of a few streets of small terrace houses built between 1827 and 1833. They were financed by industrialist Isaac Cookson to create more householders known as '40-shilling freeholders' who would qualify to vote for him at parliamentary elections. The district was named after his eldest son Arthur and some streets (now demolished) were given the names of three other sons: John, Edward and William.

4 St Paul's Church, Havelock Street

This parish church replaced a smaller chapel at Arthur's Hill (see page 24) and opened in 1859. It was designed (on a restricted budget) by John Dobson. The church is now closed but a social club continues to operate in the parish hall.

5 Elswick Lane (now Elswick Road)

Connected Elswick Township with Newcastle.

6 Barber Surgeons' Hall, Houston Street

This Italian Renaissance style, double storey building was designed by John Dobson. It opened in 1851 as 'Rye Hill College of Medicine'. The previous Barber Surgeons' Hall at Manors was required for railway development, and as compensation, the York, Newcastle and Berwick Railway funded this new accommodation. Following the College's transfer to larger premises at Orchard Street in 1863, St Paul's Church of England Primary School moved in. Sadly, this attractive building is now unoccupied following the construction of a modern primary school on an adjacent site.

The Barber Surgeons' Hall around 1924.

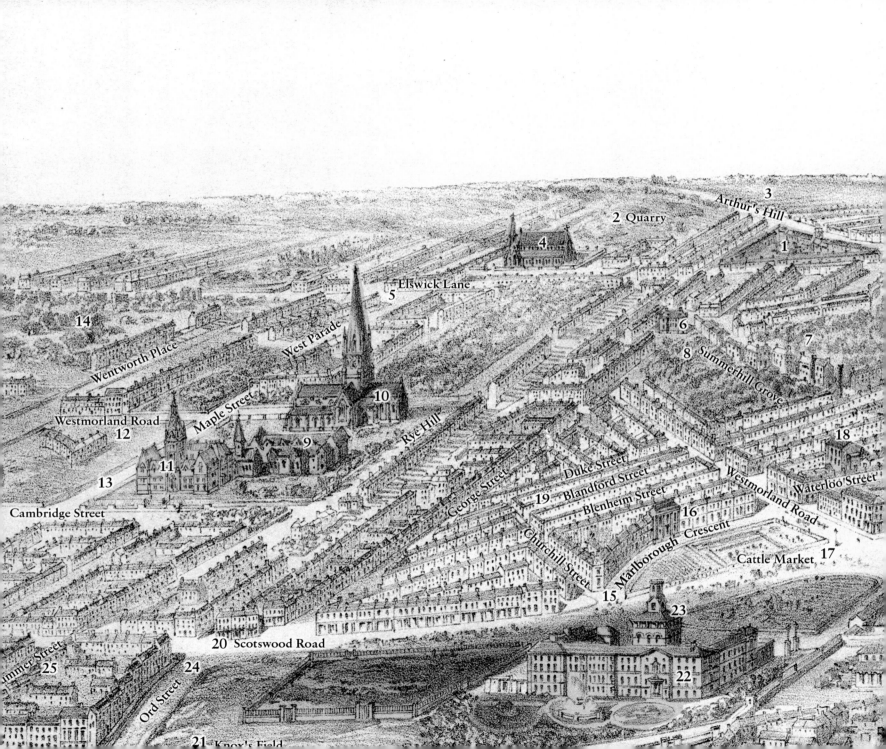

3 Arthur's Hill

2 Quarry

1

4

Elswick Lane

5

14

West Parade

6

Wentworth Place

8 Summerhill Grove

7

Maple Street

10

Westmorland Road

12

Rye Hill

9

18

11

13

Duke Street

Cambridge Street

George Street

19 Blandford Street

Westmorland Road

Waterloo Street

Blenheim Street

16

Churchill Street

Marlborough Crescent

Cattle Market

17

15

23

ummer Street

25

20 Scotswood Road

24

Ord Street

22

21 Knox's Field

7 Summerhill Park

The last will and testament of Hadwen Bragg, owner of Summerhill House (see page 24), stipulated that the adjacent land he owned was to remain undeveloped. It continues to be a pleasant open public area surrounded by 19th century housing.

8 Summerhill Grove

Built around 1825, four of these nine substantial, high-class dwellings became the home of the Richardson family – the houses had interconnecting doors. The Richardsons were well known Quakers, who operated large leather works in Newcastle. A great grandson was the late actor Sir Ralph Richardson. These houses continue to be occupied.

9, 10 St Mary the Virgin Almshouses, and Chapel

These were opened in 1858 and 1859 respectively. The land belonged to the medieval Virgin Mary Hospital which had stood more or less opposite St John's Church on Westgate Road. They were designed by the Green family of architects in the then fashionable Gothic style. The chapel became the parish church for Rye Hill in 1895 but was demolished in 1966 to make way for what is now Newcastle College.

St Mary the Virgin church, around 1925

Although dwarfed by modern College buildings, the almshouses remain in use as sheltered accommodation.

11 Royal Grammar School, Maple Street

(Some artistic licence is used here because the school was actually much nearer Westmorland Road). The school moved here in 1870 from cramped conditions at Charlotte Square. There would be space for 500 pupils including 20 boarders. The head master and his family also lived on the premises. The tuition fees were £2 5s a quarter and pupils could board at the school. There were no science laboratories, no gym and no land for outdoor games, so the school moved again in 1906 to a larger site at Jesmond. Rutherford College girls' school occupied the building until 1958, after which it was demolished. The site is now a car park.

12 Westmorland Road

Initially known as Derwent Place (1839), the street was extended westwards as Westmorland Street, Terrace, Lane and Road, eventually all consolidated into Westmorland Road. The name probably originated from the Earl of Westmorland's former medieval town house in nearby Westgate Street. The adjacent Neville Street recalls the Earl's family name.

13 Cambridge Street, Wentworth Place, West Parade, Maple Street, Rye Hill

Very little remains of the original Victorian buildings. Newcastle College now dominates the space between Maple Street and Rye Hill. Modern housing with some open grassland now covers the area.

14 Elswick Park

Originally the grounds of Elswick Hall (not included in the picture) which became a public park from 1881.

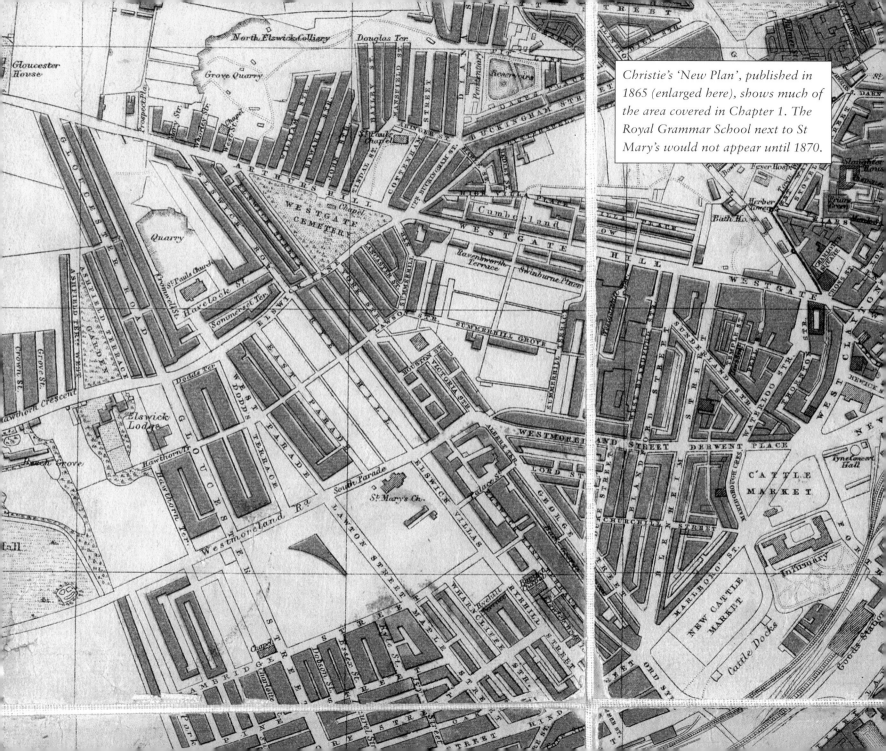

Christie's 'New Plan', published in 1865 (enlarged here), shows much of the area covered in Chapter 1. The Royal Grammar School next to St Mary's would not appear until 1870.

15 Marlborough Crescent

This elegant street was built in the early 1830s over the culverted Skinner Burn.

16 Providence Chapel, Marlborough Crescent

Brick-built in 1835 as a Baptist Chapel to seat 313 worshippers, it closed nearly 50 years later and relocated to Osborne Road in Jesmond (now demolished). A cinema, the King's Hall, opened in the former chapel in 1908 as the first permanent cinema in Newcastle. Waiting rooms were provided and bicycles stored free. In 1931 a fire destroyed the uninsured cinema. Today single-storey shops cover the site.

17 Cattle Market, Marlborough Crescent

Opened in 1830 originally for cattle, later extensions provided areas for both sheep and pigs. Later the cattle market moved to the larger Knox's field site west of the Infirmary. From the late 1920s a bus station occupied the Marlborough Crescent section for nearly 70 years. The Centre for Life complex currently covers the area.

18 Wesleyan Methodist Chapel, Blenheim Street

Completed in 1838, it marked the centenary of Methodism's foundation by John Wesley. It was built mainly of brick to seat 767 (about one half of the pews were in the galleries). A modern hotel and St James Boulevard now cover the site.

19 Blandford Street, Blenheim Street, Churchill Street, Duke Street, George Street, Sunderland Street (see Chapter 3), Waterloo Street

From 1834 John Dobson planned approximately 30 acres of land for artisan dwellings consisting of brick houses with some stone work, small gardens, back lanes and streets. Bearing in mind the 'military' nature of many of these street names, it is interesting to note that the only Newcastle soldiers to have been awarded the Victoria Cross were both born in this area. Edward Lawson was born in Blandford Street in 1873 and Adam Wakenshaw was born in Duke Street in 1914. There is a plaque to their memory at the nearby Wakenshaw VC Junction. Although much of the street layout remains, albeit modernised, there are a few original dwellings.

20 Scotswood Road

Developed in the 1830s to connect Newcastle with the recently opened Scotswood Suspension Bridge of 1831. Part of the road was initially known as West Hinde Street because it passed through the Elswick Estate belonging to John Hodgson Hinde. The name Scotswood is said to derive from a Richard Scot, who, in 1367, obtained permission to enclose a wood he owned in nearby Benwell. Though the road remains, virtually all the original buildings have been replaced with modern developments.

21 Knox's Field

William Knox, originally from Scotland, was the last farmer to work the fields in this area. He also owned a nearby flour mill and probably a pub in Forth Banks. Knox was murdered in his own field as he returned from market with the day's takings. His eldest daughter married Robert Hood Haggie, the rope manufacturer. An additional cattle market opened here, close to the railway, in 1860. After many years as a car park, the site is now covered by a modern hotel.

22 Infirmary and Gardens, Forth Banks

Essentially an accident and emergency hospital, it opened in 1753 for those too poor to be treated by doctors at home. Extensions were built at a later date and by 1859 land had been reclaimed from the Skinner Burn to form gardens containing statues and an ornamental fountain. Deteriorating

The Infirmary from the south-west in 1855.

conditions due to railway developments resulted in the opening of the Royal Victoria Infirmary at Castle Leazes in 1906. The old Infirmary buildings were demolished in 1954 and today the Centre for Life covers the site.

23 Market Keeper's House (note size exaggerated in relation to the Infirmary)

Completed in 1840 to designs by John Dobson it initially housed the families of the market manager and the toll collector. Later it became a bank and was the scene of Newcastle's first armed robbery in 1933. Now in use as commercial offices, it stands at the centre of Times Square surrounded by the Centre for Life.

24 Ord Street

The name may have a connection with the Ord family who, at one time, were land owners at Fenham.

The First Edition Ordnance Survey Map 1858-1865 shows a detailed plan of the Infirmary, its grounds, and Knox's Field just before the additional cattle market opened here in 1860.

25 Plummer Street

Probably named after the prominent Newcastle merchant family with roots dating back several centuries and after whom the Plummer Tower (on the Town Wall) and Plummer Chare (on the Quayside) were almost certainly called.

2 The Wrestling Ground to Forth Banks

1 Rail Viaduct

Designed by the Railway Company's engineer, Peter Tate, it opened in 1846 to carry the Newcastle and Carlisle Railway to a temporary terminal at Forth Banks. The low stone viaduct consists of 44 arches which continue mainly as small business units.

2 Newcastle and Carlisle Goods Station

Again designed by Tate, it opened in 1854 on a site originally acquired for Newcastle's main passenger station. In 1871 the much larger Forth Goods Station subsumed the earlier building. The site is now a combination of railway workshops, a car park and some waste land.

A wrestling match at the Wrestling Ground around 1895.

3 Wrestling Ground

From 1830 contests were held in the Cumberland and Westmorland style for prizes which, in 1857, amounted to £140. 'Wives, mothers, sisters and aunts came with the giants to applaud and encourage them in the bout by calling out the colour of their attire which they themselves had often taken pains to have conspicuous for their hero's decoration in the ring. This attire, not infrequently, might as well have

remained at home when once the couple got a hank!!' Stables were built here in around 1870 for the many horses needed by the nearby Goods Station. Today much of the site lies beneath the Redheugh Bridge (1983) approach road.

4 Pottery Lane

Once an important industrial access road, it now connects Forth Banks with the Metro Radio Arena complex at its western end. Enclosed within the area bounded by Pottery Lane, Forth Banks and the river, were several industrial businesses including the following.

1

2

9

4 Pottery Lane

Wrestling Ground

3

6 5

7

8

Forth Banks

10

5 Newcastle Pottery, Pottery Lane

Founded here before 1736 it became one of Tyneside's earliest potteries. It was only moved (to the Ouseburn) in 1893 by the then proprietors, Wallace & Co, because of imminent railway developments. Today most of the site is clear of buildings, overgrown with vegetation and awaiting development.

6 Plate Glass Works, Pottery Lane

In 1827 it is recorded that 'the cast plate glass manufactory of Messrs Isaac Cookson & Co. rivals every similar establishment in Europe in the size, fineness and brilliance of the plates produced'. The firm became R.W. Swinburne & Co. (a former Cookson's manager) employing about 600 people in 1847. It survived for nearly 50 years before going bankrupt. Plate glass, also known as 'cast glass' no longer depended on human blowing power and instead casting tables (of iron or copper plate) were used to produce ever-larger sheets of glass. The King Edward VII rail bridge

Forth Banks had become heavily industrialised by the time this photograph was taken in 1900. The 1844 map below shows the Forth recreation ground which was sited around where St Mary's Cathedral precincts and Neville Street are now. The Central Station was not yet built, but St Mary's has arrived and Neville Street will soon be widened.

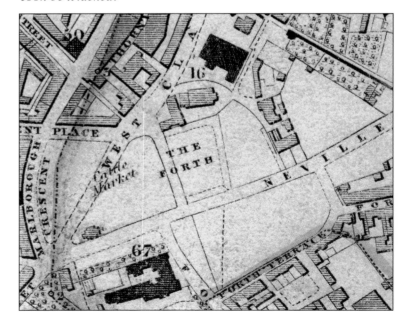

northern viaduct (opened 1906) was eventually driven through the vacant glass works site.

7 Skinnerburn Iron Works, Forth Banks

Its foundation pre-dates 1778 (Newcastle's first trade directory) when Aubone Surtees (father of Bessie Surtees, famous for her 1771 elopement) is recorded as the owner. Some late Victorian and 20th century buildings now occupy the site.

8 Northumberland Flint Glass Works, Forth Banks

The earliest trade directory entry is 1790 when John Dyson is listed as the proprietor. Initially flint glass (cut glass) was a luxury item but, during the 19th century, metallic moulds were introduced which made the products (now known as pressed flint glass) more affordable. Today the site is devoid of buildings, overgrown with vegetation and awaiting development.

9 Skinner Burn

This was the last part of the burn to be culverted and infilled (in the 1850s) which enabled the Infirmary's gardens to be extended. The Skinner Burn rose at the top end of Bath Lane and followed a meandering course under Thornton Street, Waterloo Street, Marlborough Crescent and Forth Banks before flowing into the Tyne.

10 Forth Banks

Originally linked the ancient Forth recreation area and the Infirmary with the Close and riverside.

The First Edition Ordnance Survey Map 1858-1865 gives a detailed view of the Pottery Lane area and its industry. The reservoirs are not evident on John Storey's drawing.

1 St Paul's Chapel, Arthur's Hill

When opened in 1841 it was intended to be a Chapel of Ease to St John's parish church. Fourteen years later it was sold to the Congregationalists. It became the Gem cinema in 1934, was demolished in 1967, and is now a car park. The former churchyard survives as an open public space with some headstones along one side.

2 Summerhill House

Originally built and named in the 1760s by a Newcastle bookseller, Joseph Barber, who had arrived from Summerhill, a village near Dublin. Destroyed by fire in 1773, it was rebuilt for Hadwen Bragg, a Newcastle draper. Later it became the Elswick Parsonage and, in 1887, was replaced by St Matthew's church.

3 Westgate Street (Westgate Road 1873)

One of Newcastle's earliest thoroughfares on the line of Hadrian's Wall and said, in the 1820s, 'to be chiefly inhabited by clergy and the gentry'.

4 Westgate Hill Brewery, Westgate Street

This brewery was one of many in Victorian Newcastle. Because it was on a cramped site, it used the 'tower' method of production. Today a motor cycle dealer occupies most of the former premises.

5 Bath Lane

Formerly known as Back Lane and built over the Skinner

Bath Lane, 1897. The buildings on the left are schools. Nearest to us is St John's Infant School, built in 1838 for 100 children at a penny a week. Next door is Union Girls' School which opened in 1836 for 100 girls. In the foreground is a milk delivery cart. Stowell Street leads off to the left, and Rutherford Street to the right.

Burn, it only became Bath Lane following the opening of the nearby public baths (Newcastle's first) in 1781. They consisted of 'vapour and shower baths and baths with water either in a hot, cold or tepid state besides a large open swimming basin'. The water supply eventually dried up, new public baths opened in Northumberland Road (1839) and the redundant baths were demolished before 1860.

1

2

3 Westgate Road

4

5 Bath Lane

6

7

8

9

10

11

12

13

14

Sunderland Street

Clayton Street West

15

16

17

18

19

20

21

22

23

24

Bewick Street

Neville Street

6 Tyne Brewery, Bath Lane

'One of the wonders which strangers visiting Newcastle did not fail to visit' was how the new Tyne brewery was described when it opened in 1868. It had moved from the Sandgate area of the Quayside to this greenfield site and was conspicuous by its tall central buildings, high elevators and large hoppers. Taken over by John Barras & Co. in 1884, it later became part of Newcastle Breweries. The site eventually expanded to about 22 acres but is now being redeveloped following the brewery's move to Dunston in 2005.

7 Bath House, Bath Lane

Probably built in the 1750s, its various residents include the well known Dunn family who were major contributors towards the cost of St Mary's RC Cathedral. The imposing former CWS Printing Works building (1890) now covers the site.

8 Lunatic Asylum, Bath Lane

Designed by William Newton, it opened in 1767 in 'a retired and quiet situation'. Until enlarged and improved by John Dobson nearly 60 years later, it was little more than a prison with chains and iron bars, where the sexes were occasionally mixed and where many of the dungeon-like cells were 'less comfortable than cow-houses'. A replacement institution opened in 1870 on a 57 acre site at Coxlodge, Gosforth. Nothing remains of the original asylum buildings.

9 Congregational Church, Bath Lane

John Hunter Rutherford, the son of a Scottish labourer, was so effective and popular as an evangelist that a public subscription was raised to build this church. In 1860 he became its first pastor and remained so until his death 30 years later. Built to seat 1,200 it was not unusual for more people to crowd in on special occasions. Towards the end of the 19th century Rutherford College took over much of the surrounding area. The church closed in 1939, and was demolished nearly 50 years later, but a memorial stained glass window from the church has been installed in the foyer of Northumbria University adjoining the Rutherford Hall at Ellison Place. The site is now landscaped.

10 Charlotte Square

William Newton was the architect of this high-class speculative residential development that began in 1769 on land that was once part of the Black Friars precinct. It consisted of ten substantial three-storey brick houses (with basements) built around three sides of a private central garden. Newton lived here for 20 years until his death in 1798. In the 19th century the Royal Grammar School occupied No 6 for 22 years and a synagogue occupied No 5 for 13 years. Most of the properties have survived and are commercial premises.

11 House Carpenters' Meeting Hall, Westgate Street

This two-storey stone building opened in 1812 as the meeting hall of the House Carpenters' craft guild. It replaced their previous headquarters which had been in the medieval West Gate (removed 1811) on approximately the same site. Their company arms appears on the front of the building (within the pediment) which now contains shops.

12 West Walls

This part of the medieval Town Wall is known as West Walls. The lane that ran immediately inside, and around, the wall can be seen clearly at this point, though the wall is indistinct. This lane enabled the town's defenders to move swiftly from one problem area to another. Wall construction began around 1265. It took several decades to complete and the fortifications remained in use for over 500 years. Fortunately

Newcastle retains about 10 per cent of the original two-mile Wall circuit, a high percentage for an industrial town in the UK.

13 Clayton Street West
These four-storey houses (c1837) were part of Richard Grainger's redevelopment scheme. As a widower he lived at No 36 with some of his children from 1842 to his death in 1861. He died in his office at No 28. Plaques mark each house.

14 Congregational Chapel, Clayton Street West
Built to the design of Thomas Oliver, it opened in 1851 with seating for 800. Apparently its exterior resembled a hotel and on at least one occasion a passer-by was known to have asked for a drink! A more recent building now stands on the site.

15 St Mary's Roman Catholic Cathedral and Presbytery
Father James Worswick was the mastermind behind the church (cathedral status was given in 1850). He died in 1843, a year before its completion, and was laid to rest in it 'as the church grew around him'. Renowned architect A.W. Pugin designed the building on its cramped site to accommodate 1,200 worshippers, adding a presbytery in 1858. A lack of funds prevented the tower and steeple being built then. In 1872, with help from a legacy, architects Dunn and Hansom (from the same family that created the Hansom cab) added the tower and steeple (the tallest in town at 222ft). John Storey depicts the tower and steeple in his painting.

The Tyne Concert Hall, bottom right beside the Central Station, which only existed for ten years, appears on Christie's 1865 map, but it is not included on the OS (1858-1865) map. The Forth recreation area has now disappeared.

16 John Knox Presbyterian Church, Clayton Street West
'One of Mr Dobson's happiest efforts' is how this church was described when it opened in 1854. It could accommodate 510 worshippers. The budget was limited so the church was built without a spire. The Clarendon Temperance Hotel replaced the church in 1898 and today Clarendon House (apartments over a restaurant) occupies the site.

17 Bewick Street

Named after Thomas Bewick, the renowned local wood engraver. He lived in this area for 31 years, in his 'happy little cot' (or cottage), before the new street was built in the early 1840s.

18 Forth House, Bewick Street

Reputedly an 18th century house, contemporary with that of Thomas Bewick, it was saved from demolition in 2003 and awaits development.

19 Baptist Chapel, Bewick Street

Erected in 1853 for a congregation of 850 who moved from their former chapel on Tuthill Stairs. In 1885 Bewick House replaced the chapel and today an enlarged building houses apartments over a restaurant.

20 Pink Lane

Part of the medieval thoroughfare that ran inside the Town Wall to allow for quick mobility in time of crisis. It is probably named after the Pink Tower that once stood in this area until it was demolished in 1852. It is possible that the local Spynke family financed the tower which was then named after them.

21 Neville Street

This was originally built in 1835 to connect the old meat market beyond Collingwood Street with the new cattle market (and projected railway) at Scotswood Road. It was named after the Neville family whose town house at Westmorland Place stood close by (see page 41). The street was widened for railway developments in 1847-8.

22 Tyne Concert Hall, Neville Street

This round wooden building, initially used as a Circus and then altered to become the Olympic Concert Hall, opened on

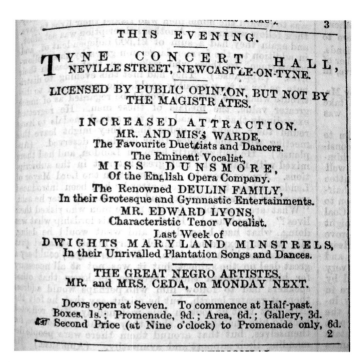

The Tyne Concert Hall advertises in the Newcastle Daily Chronicle, 21 May, 1862.

a vacant site at the west end of the Central Station in 1857. It replaced an earlier brick-built Circus and Riding School that adjoined the Forth recreation area, but was demolished in the early 1840s to make way for the new St Mary's Roman Catholic Church and Presbytery. In 1861 George Stanley, a former actor at the Theatre Royal, took over the Olympic Concert Hall and refurbished its interior 'in lavish style' with the backing of Joseph Cowen, the well known local businessman and politician. Stanley had been refused a licence to open a second theatre on the grounds that it challenged the Theatre Royal's monopoly, but he nevertheless went ahead with this project. By 1865, under its new name, the Tyne Concert Hall had become Newcastle's leading music hall. It could seat 2,500 at prices ranging from threepence to one shilling. Although alcohol was not available, smoking was permitted. Railway developments in 1866-7 forced Stanley and Cowen to move elsewhere, resulting in the building of the Tyne Theatre in Westgate Street.

23 Central Station, Neville Street

This cramped curved site provided John Dobson with a huge challenge and resulted in his most important public building and probably the climax of his career. It was opened by Queen Victoria in 1850 to service the York, Newcastle and Berwick Railway, and the Newcastle and Carlisle Railway, both of which financed its building. Dobson's techniques were later adopted at other stations. Some 45 years later, during the 1890s, the Central Station was nearly doubled in size.

The Royal Station Hotel in 1863.

24 Royal Station Hotel, Neville Street

In 1863 this new four-storey hotel opened complete with a clock tower that also contained a water tank. A six-storey hotel extension was built in 1890 together with two further storeys added to the original hotel. Because the clock tower was now concealed by taller buildings, the clocks were transferred to the station portico where they have remained.

Laing Art Gallery, Tyne & Wear Museums

The interior of the Central Station as sketched by John Dobson.

1 Hawthorn's Engine Works, Forth Banks

In 1817 Robert Hawthorn and four employees began to manufacture industrial and marine steam engines, using hand-operated machinery, in an open shed on this site. William, his brother, joined the firm later and became a partner. The business prospered in the new railway age and eventually completed over 2,600 steam locomotives (many for export) before the locomotive works were taken over by Robert Stephenson & Co. in 1937. Production ceased in 1960 and the buildings disappeared in the early 1970s in readiness for the Metro track that would emerge near here.

2 Robert Stephenson & Co., South Street

The first purpose-built locomotive works in the world was established on this eight-acre site in 1823 by Robert Stephenson, the 19-year-old son of George, who had designed and built most of the factory's machinery. *Locomotion* (1825) and *Rocket* (1829) were two of the early locomotives constructed here. The company also undertook general engineering contracts as well as marine engines and bridges. By 1860 the business had become the largest employer on Tyneside. Shortage of space and the development of larger locomotives necessitated a move to Darlington by 1902. By then the works had produced around 3000 locomotives, many for the overseas market. Subsequent occupiers of the South Street Works included motor car engineers, an aircraft manufacturer and builders' merchants. Some original buildings remain and are being cared for by the Robert Stephenson Trust.

3 Newcastle Flint Glass Works

The site is now covered by a commercial vehicle business. Flint glass is a clear glass made by a process that uses lead oxide. It was used for Newcastle Brown Ale bottles because clear glass allowed customers to see the quality of the beer within.

4 Forth Street

Originally led to the Forth recreation area from the White Friars postern (or small gateway) in the Town Wall. This postern, now covered by the Central Station, lay close to the castle and also served as an emergency exit for the castle garrison.

5 Hanover Square

Planned in the early 1700s (though never completed) on land inside the Town Wall, previously occupied by the White Friars. Hanover Square was built to cater for people moving out of the cramped, unhealthy Quayside. It was given the reigning monarch's family name. One of the first buildings, a Unitarian Chapel (1727) was replaced by a tobacco factory in the 1850s (note the chimney).

Hanover Square, 1879.

4 Forth Street

3

South Street

Orchard Street 6

7

5

2

1

8 Hanover Street

9

10

13

11

12

14

15

6 Orchard Street

Orchard Street was built on the site of a former orchard belonging to the White Friars (or Carmelites). The orchard was outside the Town Wall and could be reached through the Wall at the White Friars postern, now buried beneath the Central Station.

7 Presbyterian Church, Clavering Place

A Gothic Revival style three-storey brick building, built in 1822. It was designed by John Green for nearly 600 worshippers. Attached (to the west) is the minister's house together with vestry and schoolroom. The building has been commercially occupied since 1919.

8 Hanover Street

Contemporary with the Bonded Warehouses, this steep street connected the Close with the higher Hanover Square area. The White Friar Tower on the Town Wall, and many dwellings were demolished to build the street. It is unique because of its 'stone tramway', which provided a smooth surface for horse-drawn carts. The wheels travelled on parallel granite blocks while granite setts or cobbles between the blocks allowed the horses to walk safely on a potentially dangerous incline.

9 Bonded Warehouses, Hanover Street

These substantial brick seven-storey warehouses were built in 1841-44 to hold imported goods until duties were paid. The architect was probably Amor Spoor, a local builder, joiner and brick maker, based in Hanover Square, who lived in nearby Clavering Place. They were last used in about 1980 and recently have been severely damaged by major fires.

10 Breakneck Stairs (hidden behind buildings)

There were originally 140 steps here up to the Town Wall.

11 Closegate Bottleworks, Close

The first flint glasshouse on Tyneside was established here in 1684 outside the Closegate. Crystal drinking glasses (a marked improvement on leather or pewter) were in great demand by the merchant families. To satisfy the ever-growing demand for bottle and window glass additional glasshouses were built; they were run for a long time by the Cookson family. Today, the Copthorne Hotel more than covers the area.

12 Closegate Foundry, Close

Probably dating from the early 1700s this 'pot house and cast iron foundry' immediately outside the Close Gate was managed for several decades by the Cookson family. The site is today covered by the Copthorne Hotel.

13 Phoenix Flour Mill, Close

'One of the marvels of modern times' is how it was described at its opening in 1855. It replaced Davidson's Mill in Gateshead which was destroyed in the Great Fire the previous year. The mill was badly damaged by a bomb during World War II and the Copthorne Hotel stands on the site today.

14 Robert Brown's Steam Flour Mill, Close

Robert Brown's six-storey 'state of the art' mill opened in the mid-1850s to replace his earlier mill at Forth Banks which had been a victim of railway developments. Disaster occurred in 1866 when fire totally destroyed the property (it also caused serious damage to the woodwork of the adjacent High Level Bridge). One of the High Level's designers, Thomas Elliot Harrison (see next entry), was so concerned about the fire that he arranged a special train to take him from London to Newcastle in just five hours to inspect the bridge – incredibly fast at that time! The Fish Market building (now a night club) opened on the site in 1880.

Robert Brown's Steam Flour Mill, Close, on fire in 1866.

15 The High Level Bridge

Designed by Robert Stephenson (son of railway pioneer George) and Thomas Elliot Harrison, it became the first bridge of its type in the world with a railway on the top deck and a road underneath. Opened by Queen Victoria in 1849 it completed the rail link between London and the River Tweed. Construction by Hawks Crawshay & Sons took three years to complete and resulted in 780 families on either side of the river being re-housed, the accidental deaths of three workers, and very nearly a fourth but for his clothing catching on a protruding rivet.

The OS map (1858-1865) shows the scale of industry in this part of the town.

1 Fever Hospital (or House of Recovery), Bath Lane

Opened in 1804 'for the infected poor' on land outside the Town Wall that once belonged to the Blackfriars. Persons 'not objects of charity' were also admitted at the initial rate of two shillings per day plus

HOUSE OF RECOVERY.

the cost of their own medical attendants and medicines. The 48 original beds eventually proved inadequate and a small wooden hospital on the Town Moor (demolished 1957) served as an overflow until a Hospital for Infectious Diseases opened at Walkergate in 1888. The three-storey stone-built House of Recovery is today occupied by Museums, Libraries and Archives North East.

2 Newcastle Bowling Green, Bath Lane

Previously situated at the Forth (1657), and later in the Prudhoe Street area, it moved here in 1827. An access gateway (still visible, but now blocked) was made specially in the Town Wall. At the beginning of each season there was an annual dinner, attended by the town's dignitaries, in a nearby tavern. Closed in 1897, it became a playground for the Rutherford schools, despite having the Gallowgate Lead Works as a neighbour. Today the site consists of modern apartments, a car park, and some landscaping alongside West Walls.

3 Lead Works, Gallowgate

Begun in 1798 on a site alongside other anti-social industries (a tannery and abattoir), it always lacked good transport facilities because it was too far from the river, but managed to continue production until 1932. Instead of having the usual tower for lead shot manufacture the molten lead was dropped into a deep pit. Citygate, a modern office complex (opened 2004), now covers most of the site.

4 Stowell Street

Originally a cul-de-sac of modest two-storey terraced dwellings inside the town wall. The street was built in 1824-27 and named after locally-born Baron Stowell, the elder brother of Lord Eldon, who lived at Stowell, near Yeovil, in Somerset. This thoroughfare is now at the centre of Newcastle's Chinatown.

The Bowling Green around 1890.

1
2
3
4
5
6
7
8
9
10
11
12
13
14
15
16
17
18 Clayton Street
19
20
21
22
23
24
25
26
27 St John's Lane
28
29
30
31
32
33
34
35 Dean Street
36 Collingwood Street
37
38
39
40 Groat Market
41 Cloth Market
42
43
44
Bigg Market
Grainger Street
Nun Street
Grey Street

5 Blackfriars

Dominican friars were based here for about 300 years before Henry VIII pensioned them off and ransacked some of their buildings. Much of the site was taken over by Newcastle Corporation. It later became the HQ for some of the town's craft guilds, mostly in reconstructed buildings. Most of these buildings have now been adapted for other commercial uses.

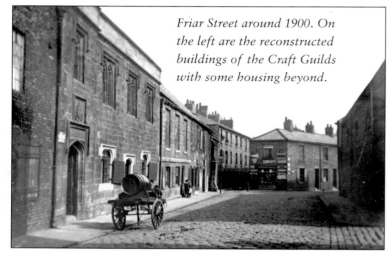

Friar Street around 1900. On the left are the reconstructed buildings of the Craft Guilds with some housing beyond.

6 Low Friar Street, (or Shod-Friar Chare)

A medieval thoroughfare marking the eastern boundary of the Blackfriars precinct and connecting the Westgate area with Newgate Street.

7 Gallowgate

Literally the street leading to the 'Town' gallows which were usually temporary structures at various sites at the edge of the Town Moor near Fenham Barracks. 'County' prisoners were generally hanged outside the West Gate.

8 Tannery, Gallowgate

Joseph Arundale, a tanner, currier and manufacturer of Morocco leather, took over this tannery in around 1820. His sister Rachel married Richard Grainger in 1821. Later, a coach station occupied this site for many years until 2003. Today much of the area, which adjoins the Town Wall at the Ever Tower, has been landscaped.

9 Public Baths and Wash-houses, Gallowgate

Built in 1857, they were Newcastle's second public baths and wash-houses but had to be demolished in 1895 when Gallowgate needed to be widened to accommodate trams. A year later they were replaced on a nearby site (demolished 1979). Eventually baths and wash-houses appeared in various districts of Newcastle.

The Public Baths and Wash-houses, Gallowgate, around 1859. St Andrew's Church and the Town Wall are on the left.

The OS map (1858-1865) shows how everything was much closer together than it seems in Storey's picture. The Gallowgate area, beyond the Town Walls, with its noxious industries, must have been very unpleasant.

10 Darn Crook (St Andrew's Street)

Its origin is uncertain but 'Darn' probably meant dark or secret – a reference to it being a dingy cul-de-sac until 1810, when the Town Wall was breached to link it with Gallowgate. 'Crook' may relate to the double bend in the course of the Lam Burn before it was culverted beneath the present street.

11 Windmill, Darn Crook

Of unknown origin, its purpose was to grind bark for use in nearby tanneries. At the tanneries the raw animal skins were steeped for up to 18 months in pits containing a concentrated solution of crushed bark to prevent decay, give them a uniform colour and to produce a leather suitable for the currier to convert into a particular end-product. Guild regulations prevented a tanner and currier doing each other's work. By 1896 the mill had become dilapidated, was demolished in the public interest and replaced by four-storey buildings with shops on the ground floor.

The windmill in Darn Crook.

12 St Andrew's Church, Newgate Street

Of uncertain foundation, it retains more of its 12th century masonry than Newcastle's other parish churches. It suffered much damage during the Civil War period (1640s) because of its vulnerable position immediately inside the Town Wall and according to the parish register: 'ther was no child baptd in this parish for 1 year's tim, after the town was taken…'

13 Strawberry Place

Laid out in the 1820s and named after Strawberry House, which stood in its own grounds opposite St James' Street. Much of the surrounding area had once been covered with nursery gardens. Few, if any, of the original buildings remain.

14 St James' Street

When built in the 1820s it was described as 'one of the most healthy, airy and retired situations in the suburb'. The adjacent football ground is said to have been named after this street. Most of the original, substantial three-storey brick terraced houses remain and are commercial offices.

15 Town Moor

The origin of this huge area of open grassland probably dates back at least to the 13th century. It has dual ownership (Newcastle City Council owns the soil and the Freemen own the grass) which, more than anything else, has preserved it. Each resident Freeman or his widow is allowed to graze two milk cows forever. In Victorian times a race track occupied a corner of the Moor – hence Grandstand Road. The races moved to Gosforth Park in 1881. Newcastle United Football Club now occupies the south-west corner of the Town Moor.

16 Newgate Street

One of Newcastle's earliest thoroughfares, it was known initially by the names of the various medieval markets held there, such as Horsemarket, Nolt (cattle) Market and White Cross. The name Newgate Street came into use from the 18th century and commemorates the strongest of the Town Wall gates (and gaol) which stood near here for over 400 years.

17 Newgate Tannery
Isaac Richardson moved here in 1800 from a tannery just outside the Pilgrim Gate. Isaac died in 1810, aged 49. To help his two infant sons, John (aged 10) and Edward (aged 4), cope with business matters, a cousin and fellow Quaker, John Priestman, became a business partner. A disastrous fire in 1863 forced a move to a purpose-built tannery at Low Elswick managed by the now adult John and Edward Richardson. The Newgate tannery site is now covered by the former Co-op department store.

18 Clayton Street
Mainly consisting of houses over shops, this final part of Grainger's re-development was completed in 1841 and named after John Clayton, Newcastle's long-serving Town Clerk who had assisted Richard Grainger in his legal transactions and in many other ways.

19 Fenkle Street
Although it appeared unnamed on a 17th century map of Newcastle, this street has had various names such as Fincle, Fennel, Charlotte and finally, Fenkle Street. Finkle and Fenkle are common street names in Northern towns and are thought to derive from a Norse word for elbow that describes a minor street with a bend. There may be a connection with a stream (now culverted) that rose near Blackfriars and flowed nearby.

20 Westgate House, Fenkle Street
This brick Georgian House (pre 1778) once belonged to the distinguished Clayton family, where father (Nathaniel) and

Cross House and Fenkle Street around 1897-8. Westgate House is the brick building on the right.

son (John) held the office of Town Clerk continuously for 82 years. The building was demolished in 1956 and today a modern office block more than covers the site.

21 Assembly Rooms, Fenkle Street
Newcastle was one of the first industrial towns to have such an elegant and sophisticated building. It was designed by local architect William Newton and opened in 1776. Fashionable society met here for dancing, cards and matchmaking in this then prosperous area of Newcastle.

22 Cross House, Westgate Street
A 17th century brick mansion which also served as St John's Vicarage for many years before being demolished in about 1900 to widen Westgate Road. The present building of reinforced concrete dates from around 1911.

The Bumler Box, Newcastle, 1866.

23 Gibb's Chambers, Westgate Street
Built in 1861 for Dr Charles John Gibb, of *Blaydon Races* fame. He lived here for 22 years and held his surgery here for 55 years. He charged a flat fee for rich or for poor patients. For night calls a speaking tube connected his bedroom to the front door. Dr Gibb was also house surgeon at the Infirmary. The building now contains offices.

24 Savings Bank, Westgate Street
Opened in 1863 on the site of St Nicholas Vicarage. Because Grainger Street West did not exist at that time, its only entrance was in Westgate Street. The facade remains but the interior has been redeveloped as a restaurant and night club.

25 St John's Works, Grainger Street West
Purpose built in 1868 for George Angus & Co, rubber merchants, it replaced their Grey Street premises which were seriously damaged by fire in the previous year. Grainger Street West was formed in 1869. Maybrook House has occupied the site since 1971.

26 Bumler Box, St John's Lane
This curious structure likened to 'Noah's Ark' or 'Hancock's Birdcage' was originally part of an old tannery. Low roofed, springless carriages were known locally as 'Bumler Boxes'. The name may also derive from dialect for a small house, or for a box to hold bees. Later it became an oilcloth factory until developments in the late 1860s caused its demise.

27 St John's Lane
Developed in 1784 to link Bigg Market with Westgate Street, it required the removal of part of the churchyard and the shortening of the north aisle of St John's church. Regarded as 'a narrow dirty place' and nicknamed 'Copper Alley'

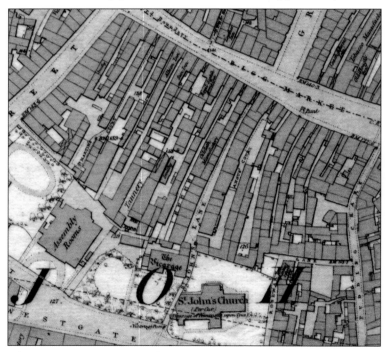

The OS map (1858-1865) shows the narrow St John's Lane and Vicarage Gardens which were to be replaced by the 1863 Savings Bank.

(workmen's wages were paid in copper) it was widened eventually to form Grainger Street West in 1869.

28 St John's Church, Westgate Street
One of Newcastle's four parish churches and essentially 15th century with later restorations. It has an anchorage, the cell of a religious recluse who spent their life behind a door locked by the Bishop. A pierced cross in a wall allowed the anchorite to watch the celebration of Mass at the altar. It can still be seen.

29 George Stephenson's Monument, Westgate Street (see page 13)
Unveiled in 1862, partially on the site of the former medieval hospital of St Mary the Virgin. The bronze statue of the railway pioneer is surrounded by four seated figures said to represent significant aspects of his career.

Westmorland Place, on the right, around 1860, before the Mining Institute (Neville Hall) was built to change the view entirely. The Lit and Phil, with its roof lights, can be seen just behind Westmorland Place.

30 Temperance Hotel, Westgate Street
This former Temperance Hotel and Family Boarding House was replaced in 1866 by the Newcastle Chronicle Printing Works and Offices.

31 Westmorland Place, Westgate Street
Once the spacious and elegant 14th century town house of the powerful Neville family, it was replaced in 1872 by the present Neville Hall.

32 Literary and Philosophical Society, Westgate Street
Opened in 1825, on part of the gardens and outhouses of Westmorland Place, as a centre for intellectual and cultural activities. It possessed (and still does) an important library before public libraries were commonplace. John Green, the architect, designed the building in the Greek Revival style.

33 Museum and School of Design
Planned to house the natural history collection, it opened in 1836 on land at the rear of the Literary and Philosophical Society. It was designed by John and Benjamin Green. Later it also held the Fine Arts Society's collection. In 1884 the premises were demolished for railway expansion.

34 School of Medicine
John Dobson designed this building in the garden behind

Westmorland Place. The medical school moved here in 1852 from the Barber Surgeons' Hall at Manors, because of railway developments. For the same reason the school was obliged to leave for Castle Leazes 37 years later.

35 Dean Street

When constructed in the 1780s over the Lort Burn ravine it became the town's first bypass, and provided an alternative to the congested Pilgrim Street or Side for people travelling between the Quayside and upper Newcastle. A few of the original brick houses over shops remain.

36 Collingwood Street

Opened 1810 with 'handsome three storey brick houses over elegant shops', which were 'generally considered by visitors to be as excellent as any outside London' and named after Trafalgar hero Admiral Cuthbert Collingwood, who was born nearby. The original buildings have all been replaced by later structures.

37 St Nicholas' Church, St Nicholas Street

Its architecture is mainly 14th and 15th century with more recent restorations. It is probably the second or third church on the site. The outstanding feature is its splendid lantern tower which acted as an inland lighthouse, with coal burning in a brazier, for travellers arriving by river or overland. Its cathedral status (Anglican) dates from 1882.

38 Mosley Street

Once the fashionable and commercial heart of Newcastle, in around 1880 it became the first street in the UK to be lit with electricity. Built a century earlier, originally with mainly three-storey brick houses over shops (only one remains), it was named after local businessman Edward Mosley who financed much of its construction.

39 Town Hall, Mosley Street

Completed in 1863, it contained Council offices, a public concert hall to seat 3,000, a hotel, several shops and a bank. Replaced by the Civic Centre at Barras Bridge, the Victorian buildings were demolished in 1973 and the site redeveloped.

40 Groat Market

Originally the medieval oatmeal (groats) market, it had its share of dwellings, pubs and coaching inns. Also here were Newcastle's first Assembly Rooms and a Presbyterian Chapel.

41 Cloth Market

Another medieval market area where two multi-day fairs were held each year. Wealthy merchants lived here until the 17th century when it became the Flesh Market. Following the removal of the Meat Market, nearly two centuries later, it was renamed Cloth Market.

42 Bigg Market

From an early date this became the barley market (Bygg is a Scandinavian word for barley) and not surprisingly a centre for pubs and coaching inns.

43 Grainger Street

One of Richard Grainger's new streets, constructed in the late 1830s and named after him. Never intended as a main thoroughfare, it only developed as such because the major railway station had its situation at the end of the street.

44 Nun Street

Another of Richard Grainger's new streets covering part of the 11th century St Bartholomew's Nunnery which stood here for about 450 years.

Charles Humble's basket shop, Cloth Market, around 1862. The houses were demolished in 1863 and are not in the panorama. A knife grinder stands outside. The shop behind Humble's was occupied by J. Nixon, hair curler and perfumer. The tower of the new Town Hall nears completion behind the shops.

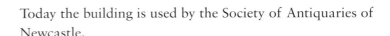

1 St Nicholas Building, St Nicholas Street

Built in around 1851 following the opening of the High Level Bridge. Although intended as office accommodation (which it still is), it did contain the *Newcastle Chronicle* printing works for three years until Joseph Cowen moved to purpose-built premises at Westgate Street in 1866.

2 Railway Bridge over St Nicholas Street

A plaque on the south side of the bridge, which carries the east coast main line between London and Scotland, records its construction in 1848 by J. Abbot & Co. at their Park Iron Works, Gateshead. It was later doubled in width.

3 Castle Keep, Castle Garth

Now Newcastle's oldest building, dating back to the 12th century, it was once part of the three-acre castle complex built on the site of the Roman Fort (Pons Aelius). In 1080 the Normans established their wooden motte and bailey castle here and named it the New Castle. The castle, including the Keep, was completely rebuilt in stone some 90 years later.

4 Black Gate, Castle Garth

This originated as a barbican, or extra fortification, added to the castle's most vulnerable side in 1247. Following the end of Scottish hostilities in the early 1600s, a speculator named Patrick Black added storeys of brick and transformed it into tenement dwellings.

Today the building is used by the Society of Antiquaries of Newcastle.

5 Castle Garth

Generally defined as the three-acre area within the 12th century castle walls. From 1400, because the King wished to continue his control of the royal castle, the garth remained legally part of Northumberland within an independent Newcastle. From the 1600s it gradually became crowded with unsavoury tenements and a haven for illegal trades. It was cleared in the early 19th century and landscaped in more recent times.

6 Moot Hall, Castle Garth

Completed in 1812, the building served as the Northumberland County Court and Prison. Designed by John Stokoe in the Greek Revival style, it remains in use as a Crown Court.

The Dean Street arch around 1860.

7 Side

Formerly a medieval residential and shopping thoroughfare by the 'side' of the castle. Before the 1780s it was one of only two routes (the other was via Pilgrim Street) a traveller would use to and from Newcastle's only bridge.

8 Railway Bridge over Dean Street

Opened in 1848 to connect the Newcastle and Berwick Railway line from Manors Station to the Central

1

2

3

4

5 Castle Garth

6

7 Side

8

9

10 Close

11

12

13

14

15

16

Station and so to the High Level Bridge. Its width was doubled nearly 50 years later.

9 Castle Stairs

Of medieval origin, they provided access between the Quayside and Castle Garth. They were 'lined on both sides with clog shops' and reckoned to be the centre of Newcastle's boot trade. The shops have now gone but the stairs remain.

10 The Close

One of the oldest streets in Newcastle and originally much narrower or enclosed. Many of the town's principal inhabitants lived here in impressive homes with rooms described as 'very large and stately', until industrialisation in the late 1700s forced them to move away, generally uphill, to less polluted, much quieter and less crowded residential areas.

11 Toll House, Close

Built in the 1860s, it was one of several toll houses around the edge of Newcastle to collect the 'Thorough Toll' a medieval tax levied on all goods entering or leaving the town as a contribution towards highway maintenance. Following the toll's abolition in 1910, this two-storey stone building served as a coroner's court (with mortuary) and more

Newcastle Quayside from Gateshead around 1863.
The Georgian bridge would survive for a few more years.
Note the fire-damaged Gateshead shore.

recently as a medical centre for the homeless. Currently the building accommodates offices.

12 Tyne Bridge (Georgian)

Opened in 1781 it replaced the medieval bridge (with its houses and shops) which had survived for over 500 years until severely damaged during a major flood in 1771. Widened in c.1802, it was replaced by the Swing Bridge (opened in 1876) which allowed larger vessels to pass up and down stream.

13 Sandhill

At one time it was the open sandy, tidal mouth of the Lort Burn. Land reclamation and culverting in the 1300s created an enlarged thoroughfare around which buildings were erected. For centuries it was the centre of the town's business and social life which included markets, craft guild plays, bull baiting and public executions.

14 Bessie Surtees House, Sandhill

This timber-framed five-storey house (now English Heritage) was typical of a merchant or businessman's property in the 17th century. Such an unusually large amount of expensive glass was, in itself, an indicator of significant wealth at this time. It was from this building in 1772 that Bessie Surtees eloped with locally born John Scott, later to become Lord

Chancellor of England and eventually Lord Eldon. He adopted the title Eldon from the County Durham village near Bishop Auckland.

15 The Guildhall, Sandhill

Civic headquarters have occupied this important site next to the busy quayside and bridge since medieval days. At that time it also included an almshouse for some of the town's poor and needy. The building visible today dates from the 1650s together with a major refacing of the exterior some 150 years later, and includes a court and meeting rooms. The building today contains offices including the Visitor Information Centre.

16 Ye Old Queene Elizabeth Inn, Quayside

Once the home of 17th century Newcastle merchant and alderman John Cosyn, it later became an eating house and finally an inn. Although it survived the Great Fire of 1854, it was demolished in 1890. Thirty years later the site was required for the foundations of the new Tyne Bridge.

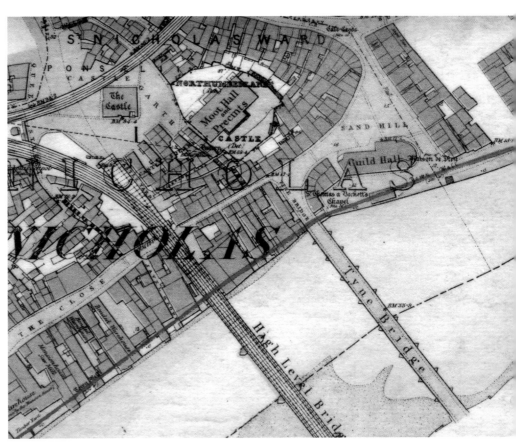

The OS map (1858-1865) shows the relationship between the Keep and the Moot Hall. Note the empty area right of Sandhill where there was fire damage.

Left, Ye Old Queene Elizabeth Inn shortly before its demolition. It gives an impression of the old Quayside.

7 Chimney Mills to the Royal Arcade

1 Leazes Terrace
These three-storey stone-fronted homes (59 in total) were described as 'one of the finest terrace developments in England' following their completion in 1834. Designed by the well-known Newcastle architect, Thomas Oliver, they attracted wealthier occupants with their healthy situation, internal water supply, front gardens with railings and decorative cast-iron balconies. Many have now been converted into students' accommodation.

2 Leazes Park
Originally part of the Town Moor, it became Newcastle's first public park in 1873. It had croquet greens, tennis courts and two lakes to provide healthy recreation for people living in the town. The word 'leazes' is derived from the Old English for a pasture or meadow.

3 Leazes Crescent
Brick-built and faced with stucco, these two-storey terraced cottages were designed by Thomas Oliver in 1829-30.

4 Albion Place
Described initially as 'a row of convenient houses facing St James's Street across gardens and shrubberies', these three-storey brick terrace houses were built in around 1810. Now renamed Leazes Park Road.

5 St Thomas's Crescent
These modest brick terrace houses were part of a piecemeal development completed about 1862 by an unknown architect. At the time that Storey was working on his view of Newcastle, the artist William Bell Scott (1811-1890) was living at 14 St Thomas's Crescent. D.G. Rossetti visited there in 1862. A plaque records Bell Scott's residence in the street.

6 St Thomas's Street
More modest brick terrace houses, again by an unknown architect, completed about 1842.

7 Percy Street
Formerly known as Sidgate (the street leading to the Side) it lay outside the Town Wall and consisted 'of houses very indifferent, most of which are inhabited by poor people but very sweetly situated having the Leazes or Gardens behind them'. The street was renamed in honour of the Percy family in the mid-18th century.

8 Percy Iron Works

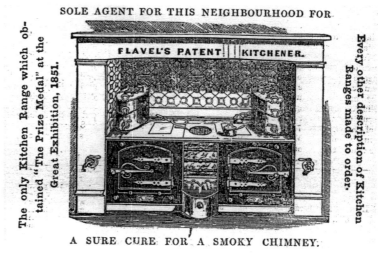

A speciality of the Percy Iron Works, advertised in 1855.

1
2
3
4
5
6
8
9
11
12
13
10
7 Percy Street
14 Haymarket
15
16
63
61
62
21 22 17
23
25
24
18
28
26
27
36
60
59
19
20
31
30
35
34
33
37
51 52
53
54
55
50
56
29
32
Grey Street
Pilgrim Street
49
44
45
48
43
58
38
46
40
47
42
Trafalgar Street
64
39
41
57

9 Bruce's Academy, Percy Street

Founded by John Bruce in 1806 partially on the site of a non-conformist burial ground, this private school closed in 1881 and a laundry occupied the building until Newcastle Breweries re-developed the area several years later.

10 Crow's Nest Public House, Percy Street

Newcastle Breweries rebuilt the present Crow's Nest Building in around 1900 on the site of an earlier three-storey brick mansion known as Crow Trees. A few trees where birds nested lay in between this mansion and the adjacent lower level Crow's Nest pub, long since demolished.

11 Lax's Gardens

Originally nursery gardens worked by William Lax, a farmer living close by in Vine Lane.

12 Chimney Mills, Claremont Road

Just one of Newcastle's many windmills, it opened in 1782. It was designed by John Smeaton, the celebrated English engineer (better known for his rebuild of the Eddystone Lighthouse) and was the first to have five sails.

13 Eldon Place and Street

Only a few of the town houses that once lined this thoroughfare overlooking the nursery gardens survive. George and Robert Stephenson, the railway pioneers, lived here for a short while during the 1820s. Newcastle University buildings now dominate the area.

14 Haymarket

Before 1808 it was described as a 'dirty, unseemly waste, with many putrid pools, offensive to senses and injurious to health'. It then became a parade ground for the inspection of the Newcastle Volunteers, followed in 1824 by an open-air hay and straw market. A bus station was built here in 1930.

15 Barras Bridge

Once carrying the Great North Road over the Pandon Burn, the bridge now lies beneath the road. It is thought the name 'Barras' is derived from the barrows or burial mounds of lepers from the nearby Mary Magdalene Hospital.

16 St Thomas's Church, Barras Bridge

Opened in 1830 and designed by John Dobson. It replaced the medieval chapel of St Thomas the Martyr which stood for centuries at the north end of the old Tyne Bridge where travellers would leave a donation and say a prayer for a safe crossing. The church on Barras Bridge never became a parish church with a vicar; instead it supported a master who became chaplain to various institutions including the universities. The Metro and Victoria Tunnels both pass underground nearby.

17 Blackett Street

Richard Grainger built this new street of 31 brick houses over shops during the three-year period beginning in 1824. They were built to a design by Thomas Oliver on waste land previously outside the Town Wall. The street was named after John Erasmus Blackett, merchant and hostman, father-in-law of Admiral Cuthbert Collingwood, four times mayor of Newcastle and the last Blackett to hold public office in the town. All of these buildings were demolished in the 1960s to make way for the new Eldon Square shopping complex.

18 Old Eldon Square, Blackett Street

Completed by Richard Grainger to Thomas Oliver's and John Dobson's design in 1831, it consisted of 26 high-class

Reid's map of 1878 shows the relationship between the streets and buildings which are out of proportion on the picture. By 1878 the site of the new Free Library was earmarked on New Bridge Street, and Leazes Park had become a public park. Lax's nursery gardens are above Percy Street.

terraced stone houses with small gardens and railings at the front, around three sides of an open square. It had been intended to place a statue of Lord Eldon at the centre of the square but instead a war memorial was unveiled in 1923. Two sides of the square were demolished in the 1960s to make way for the new Eldon Square shopping complex.

19 St James' Chapel, Blackett Street
Designed by John Dobson and opened as a Presbyterian Church in 1826 to seat 600. The building was extended 33 years later, by which time it had become a Congregational Church. The congregation moved in 1884 to Northumberland Road as St James' United Reformed Church and the Blackett Street building was sold to the YMCA. Today the site has become an entrance to the Eldon Square shopping complex.

20 United Presbyterian (Scotch) Church, Blackett Street
Completed around 1822 by John and Benjamin Green, and rebuilt in 1858, it provided a place of worship for nearly 650 Presbyterians. In 1904 it was replaced by the resplendent Emerson Chambers which opened as shops and offices over a high-class restaurant with a resident orchestra. The church moved to Northumberland Road as Trinity Presbyterian Church and is today part of Northumbria University.

21 High Friar Street
The Franciscan (or Grey) Friars had their 13th century friary at the east end of this street which is now largely covered by the Eldon Square shopping complex.

22 High Friar Lane
Richard Grainger was born in 1797 in an upstairs two-room tenement and though the original buildings have been demolished, part of the lane remains off Pilgrim Street.

BLACKETT STREET UNITED PRESBYTERIAN CHURCH, NEWCASTLE-ON-TYNE.
The ANNUAL SOIREE of the Congregation will be held in the Lecture Hall of the Church, on WEDNESDAY, the 31st inst. Tea on the tables at 5 o'clock. Tickets, 1s. each, may be had of Messrs. HORN and STORY, Grey Street; JAMES DUNLOP, 107, Clayton Street; SNOWBALL and ALLEN, Northumberland Street; and BERTRAM BROTHERS, Bigg Market.
A STALL for the Sale of Useful and Ornamental Needlework, &c. (in aid of the City Mission Fund in connection with the Congregation,) will be open during the day from 11 o'clock till 3, in the Lecture Hall of the Church. The Sale will be resumed again at the Soiree, in the evening.

THIS EVENING.
LITERARY & PHILOSOPHICAL SOCIETY, NEWCASTLE-UPON-TYNE.
D. PAGE, Esq., F.G.S., Edinburgh, will Deliver TWO LECTURES, MONDAY, JAN. 29, and WEDNESDAY, JAN. 31. Subject:—"The Ocean, its Physical Characteristics and Functions."
R. C. CLAPHAM, } Hon Secs.
R. S. WATSON, }
Each Lecture will commence at 7·30 p.m.   1110

A Soirée at Blackett Street United Presbyterian Church, and a lecture at the Lit and Phil are advertised for 31 January, 1866.

St James' Chapel in its role as the YMCA around 1885.

23 Green Court

An uncovered vegetable market operated here from about 1838 because the main site at the nearby Grainger Market, opened three years earlier, was proving to be too small. A purpose-built covered vegetable market opened in 1875 on an adjoining larger site and Green Court was transformed into St Andrew's Street.

24 Nelson Street

Completed during the late 1830s as part of Grainger's redevelopment programme, it contained some public buildings including the Music Hall, the Dispensary and a Primitive Methodist Chapel.

25 Grainger Market

Designed by John Dobson to contain 188 butchers' shops and 55 fruit and vegetable dealers, all under cover, it was 'considered the most spacious and magnificent in Europe', when it opened in 1835. A nunnery had stood on the site until the 16th century.

26 Brunswick Methodist Chapel, Brunswick Place

Opened in 1821 as successor to the Orphan House on Northumberland Street (see below), which was now too small, this brick building became the mother church of Methodism in the North East of England and could seat nearly 1,400. Worshippers here have included Emerson Muschamp Bainbridge (treasurer for 33 years) John James Fenwick (Circuit Steward and Sunday School Superintendent) and Richard Grainger (Sunday School teacher). The chapel was named after Caroline of Brunswick, Queen Consort of King George IV.

27 Coach building factory, Elswick Court

'Two splendid railway coaches' were built here for the

The top of Grey Street around 1860.

Khedive of Egypt only to find they were too wide to be moved out of the works – they had to be partially dismantled and re-assembled. Fenwick's department store eventually took over the factory site.

28 Prudhoe Street

Opened in 1822 to connect Percy Street with Northumberland Street. The construction of the Eldon Square shopping complex in the 1960s resulted in its demise.

29 Grey Street

Grey Street has earned many accolades over the decades for its spectacular classical architecture since its completion in about 1839. It is a broad and descending thoroughfare with 'a subtle curve'. It never became the town's main shopping street as intended, largely because the railway station, when it was needed ten years later, could not be sited at its foot due to the lack of level ground. The street was designed by various architects and built mainly as houses over shops from high quality sandstone. It was constructed over the 'vast nauseous hollow' of the Lort Burn, part of which had been the site of an open-air butchers' market. Initially named Upper Dean Street, it became Grey Street a few years later.

30 Central Exchange

Corn merchants and farmers had long requested an indoor market in Newcastle. Richard Grainger offered the interior of this large triangular building free of charge to the corporation. The offer was refused because a corn market was already being planned opposite St Nicholas' Church in Mosley Street. Instead the large interior became a spacious, elegant newspaper reading room which opened in 1839. Newspapers at this time were relatively expensive to buy due to a Government tax that was not repealed until the mid 1850s, but they could be read here by gentlemen (ladies were not permitted) in return for an annual subscription of £1 1s. Over 40 years later, an art gallery opened alongside the news room, which was used for exhibitions, social gatherings, and concerts. There were separate rooms for activities such as chess, card games, billiards and smoking. A vaudeville theatre and restaurant replaced the art gallery in 1897, though the newspaper reading rooms were retained. A disastrous fire occurred in 1900, resulting in the complete

An exhibition at the Central Exchange in around 1863.

destruction of the interior of the building (essentially timber). The fire began in the early hours of the morning which meant there was no loss of life though about 70 people became unemployed. In 1906 the present shopping arcade opened, complete with outstanding glazed coloured tiles and spacious lofty basements. The exterior of the Central Exchange consisted mainly of houses over shops but also included dining rooms and a coffee house which, from the early 1850s, formed part of a new hotel on the upper floors.

31 Grey's Monument

Charles, Earl Grey, the only Northumbrian to have been Prime Minister won national acclaim in 1832 for supporting the move towards Parliamentary reform. Local people felt he should be commemorated with a monument and among the various sites suggested were the Town Moor and North Shields. Completed in 1838, during Earl Grey's lifetime, the monument was financed by public subscription and designed by John and Benjamin Green. Earl Grey is now probably better remembered for the tea that bears his name.

32 Bank of England, Grey Street
Probably designed by John Wardle, one of an important group of talented and contemporary architects, the style is that of an Italian Renaissance palace. A restaurant now occupies the premises.

33 Theatre Royal, Grey Street
John and Benjamin Green designed this second Theatre Royal to replace an earlier structure at the foot of, and obstructing, what is now Grey Street. At its opening in 1837, church bells rang. Seats were priced at three shillings for a box, two shillings for a moveable seat in the pit, one shilling in the gallery, to watch Shakespeare's *The Merchant of Venice*. Improvements and restorations have been made over the years and at the moment seating capacity is almost 1,300.

Contemporary with and alongside the theatre, Shakespeare Street originally accommodated houses over shops on both sides of the street until the theatre interior was re-designed after a major fire in 1900.

34 Market Street
Another of Grainger's streets, it was completed around 1837 and led to the popular Grainger Market which had opened two years earlier.

35 Hood Street
Named after John Lionel Hood, a hostman and the last mayor of Newcastle before the major reorganisation of the Town Corporation in 1835. It contained houses over shops as well as a Salem Chapel, again to the plan of Richard Grainger.

Grey Street, 1870, graciously ascends towards the Theatre Royal and Grey's Monument above the 'nauseous hollow' of the culverted Lort Burn.

36 Northumberland Street
For most of Newcastle's existence this street led directly to Northumberland and beyond. For a long time it was a residential suburb lying outside the Town Walls. By 1736 it was described as 'a very well built street, having in it some very pretty houses standing in the middle of gardens and shady fields'. The opening of J.J. Fenwick's ladies' outfitter's shop in 1882, with a staff of two, marked its transition into the commercial thoroughfare it is today.

37 Orphan House School (Wesleyan), Northumberland Street
This school opened in 1857 on the site of an earlier Orphan House or Methodist Chapel opened by John Wesley in 1743. The Orphan House was named after a similar institution founded in 1698 at Hayle in Cornwall for 'the instruction of poor children', who may or may not have been orphans – it

later looked after neglected people rather than solely orphaned children.

In Newcastle's Orphan House of 1743, the chapel occupied the ground floor, with classrooms and a band room on the first floor and on the second floor, were apartments for visiting preachers and their families. Wesley's rooms were in a small wooden building on the roof. He made use of

John Storey made this drawing of the Orphan House before it was replaced in 1857 by the building depicted in the panorama.

them on his many visits to Newcastle throughout his long and active life. Brunswick Chapel opened nearby in 1821 to cope with an increased Wesleyan congregation. The Orphan House School of 1857 offered basic education until the Board Schools emerged later in the century. It later had various functions, including that of a YMCA hostel until finally demolished in 1955. A circular plaque by a shop doorway indicates the site of the school.

38 Royal Arcade, Pilgrim Street

John Dobson designed this imposing stone building and intended it to be Newcastle's first indoor corn market or exchange. The Corporation had other ideas so the plan was rejected. Instead, when it opened in 1832, it became a shopping arcade (which eventually was to include banks, a post office, and even a steam and vapour bath) with offices

The Royal Arcade around 1840.

above. Ultimately the building proved to be a white elephant, because it was too far from the town's new developments and railway station, but too close to unsavoury areas at its rear. In the 1960s the building was removed for motorway development (the Pilgrim Street roundabout now covers the site) and a plan to re-construct the Arcade elsewhere at a later date never came to pass. Much of the stone was recycled or used in local parks as benches.

39 Holy Jesus Hospital, Manors

Built as an almshouse partly on the site of the former Augustinian Friary, it opened in 1681 to provide single-room accommodation for some of the town's poor Freemen or their widows, or their unmarried children. This narrow three-storey brick building containing 42 small rooms, all facing south, was funded by the Corporation who insisted on vetting all applicants. Originally all inmates received an annual allowance of £4, raised eventually to £13, at which point they became entitled to an annual supply of the 'best Benwell coals' as well as some clothing, all at the Corporation's expense. The almshouse closed in 1937 when replacement bungalows were opened at Spital Tongues. Today the National Trust occupies the building.

40 Rail Terminus and Coal Depot, Carliol Square

A temporary terminus for the new Newcastle and North Shields Railway opened here in 1839. It was intended to extend the line to a permanent passenger station in Pilgrim Street but this never happened. Initially there were no passenger facilities but after some delay and uncertainty as to where permanent stations would be sited, it was decided to build a single-storey stone booking office which could also serve as a waiting room. A decade later, Manors Passenger Station opened nearby and from then onwards the temporary terminus served as a coal depot and, more recently, as a small

Travelling in style in First Class on the Great Northern Railway. From the Illustrated London News, 22 November, 1879.

bus station. The 1970s motorway now covers the site.

It is worth recalling what rail travel was like in the early days. A helping hand from other waiting passengers might be needed for the steep, two-step climb into the carriages. A rope hung from the door as another aid. While first-class carriages were covered, with a door at each end, the other trucks were open to the elements. Seats ran down each side of the truck and another back-to-back row of benches with a backrest between them ran down the centre. Smoking was banned on trains following some early fire damage, but in 1868 railway companies were legally obliged to provide smoking areas on every train containing more than one carriage of each class, unless they were exempted by the Board of Trade.

Single fares for the full seven mile journey to North Shields were: First Class one shilling, Second Class ninepence and Third Class sixpence, with proportionately reduced fares for intermediate station travel.

41 Gas Works, Manors

Newcastle's second gas works for the manufacture of coal gas opened here in 1823 to augment the town's first works which had begun at Forth Street in 1817. They both closed following the development of a larger site at Low Elswick in 1859. (For more about the manufacture of coal gas see page 94.)

42 Passenger Railway Station, Manors

This small, but distinguished-looking Renaissance style building with unusually elaborate chimneys opened next to the gas works in 1849 as Newcastle's first permanent passenger station. John Dobson was the architect. It became the terminus of the Newcastle Berwick railway for about a year, until the Central Station opened in 1850. Demolished in

1907, the site today is covered by Manors multi-storey car park.

43 Croft Street

Carliol Croft was a long garden and orchard, immediately inside the eastern edge of the medieval Town Wall. It extended for about 400 yards south from what is now New Bridge Street (near the former Carliol Tower) to the Manors area (alongside the Austin Tower). The Croft belonged to the Carliol family who had been wealthy local merchants and politicians in the 13th century and were said to have been the founders of the nearby Franciscan Friary. An early local historian recalls 'the footpath next the wall formed an agreeable walk, presenting a prospect of the gardens on the west, the Windmill Hills and the adjacent country' and 'this walk was generally frequented in a summer's evening by the gentry of this part of the town'. The present street is only half of its original length but nevertheless follows the line of that early footpath.

At the foot of the street is Plummer Tower. This is one of the 17 towers which formed part of the medieval Town Wall. It was probably paid for by the Plummer family, another of Newcastle's prominent merchant and political families. The Guild of Masons eventually occupied the premises as their headquarters and in 1742 they rebuilt the facade in the fashionable style, which included an elaborate Venetian window. Later uses of the building have been varied and today they are occupied as offices.

Just above the tower is the Royal Improved School for Girls. This plain single-storey brick building (70 x 30ft), by an unknown architect, opened in 1814 at the initiative of a committee of ladies under the patronage of the Duchess of Northumberland. About 200 girls were given a very basic

education plus needlework at a cost of a penny per week by monitors or helpers. They were usually older children who had already been instructed by the only teacher. They went on to assist her to cope with so many girls. The

The girls' school in its early years.

school closed in the late 19th century and today the site has been completely redeveloped.

44 Erick Street

The Erick Burn, another of Newcastle's several streams, originally defined the western edge of Carliol Croft and had been culverted as early as 1733 to form the street.

45 Carliol Street

Following the development of the Carliol Croft area, around 1820, this became another street of dwellings that included a Presbyterian Chapel. All the original buildings have now disappeared, although a small part of the street remains as a busy thoroughfare.

46 Carliol Square

Formed in the late 1820s, around the gaol, it is today a cul-de-sac since the opening of the motorway.

47 Gaol, Carliol Square

Newcastle's earlier gaol, at Newgate, was demolished in 1823 as part of the Town Wall clearance programme. It was replaced five years later by this new prison which was said to resemble a feudal fortress. John Dobson's innovative design was semi-circular in shape with blocks of cells radiating from a guardroom, all enclosed within an 26ft-high wall. The Prison Inspectorate later found fault with this radial layout so in the 1860s Dobson replaced it with a new design for a single block, containing prisoners' cells.

Cells at this time were tiny, unlit after dusk, and contained little more than a plank bed. Mattresses could be earned as a privilege for good behaviour. Up to 300 prisoners, most serving sentences of two years or less, could be housed. They included debtors and children. Punishments, such as the treadmill and flogging were gradually being phased out. In total 14 executions took place here, all for murder. In the early years they were public executions, but after 1868 they took place within the walls. At the last public execution, in 1863, a 19-year-old was hanged on top of the prison wall and 'the whole thoroughfare had the appearance of a street paved with human heads'. People assembled as early as 5.30am, some two-and-a-half hours ahead of the hanging. 'The crowd was so dense that dozens of people fainted, who were then passed over the heads of the multitude to the outside'.

The prison closed in 1925 and was replaced by a telephone exchange. The high quality sandstone was recycled and can be seen in various places, including the church of St James and St Basil at Fenham, and the approach to the Tyne Bridge at the Gateshead end.

48 Clergy Jubilee School, Carliol Square
The school's foundation in 1819 commemorated the 50th anniversary of Shute Barrington, Bishop of Durham. Designed by John Dobson, it did not open until 1821 because of lack of funds. The nearby St Nicholas' Charity School (later Dame Allan's Endowed Schools) financed the completion of the building on condition that its free scholars

could transfer from their existing building in Manor Chare.

Eventually fee-paying pupils, at a penny a week (except for orphans and children of widows), plus the free scholars from

The Clergy Jubilee School around 1821.

the Charity School, totalled on average 400 boys and girls who were taught the three Rs in two separate rooms, the boys at ground level and the fewer girls on the floor above. The annual salary of the boys' master was £80 plus accommodation and coal, with the girls' mistress earning £40 annually plus accommodation and coal. Monitors or helpers acted as teachers. They were usually older pupils from the charity school, who could earn a shilling per week plus an annual bonus of up to £4. St Nicholas' Charity School moved to Rosemary Lane in 1860 and the old building became the Clergy Jubilee Trades School until its closure in 1938.

49 RC Chapel and School, Carliol Square
By building a chapel in the lengthy back garden of his Pilgrim Street home in 1798, James Worswick, a Roman Catholic priest, was able to conduct the first public High Mass in Newcastle for about 250 years. A school for boys and girls was added later. As a result of town developments in the 1870s, Worswick Street was created on the site of Worswick's property and a replacement church, St Andrew's, opened in 1875. Worswick was also the driving force behind the construction of St Mary's Roman Catholic Church at

Clayton Street West (see page 27). He died (and was interred there) a year before its completion in 1844.

50 New Bridge Street
Created around 1812 on the line of the Town Wall, following its removal between Pilgrim Gate and Carliol Tower. The New Bridge over Pandon Dene, which also opened in that year, enabled the street to be extended eastwards towards the developing suburbs.

51 Trinity Presbyterian Church, New Bridge Street
Designed in the Early English style by John Dobson and opened in 1847, it was somewhat ornate for a dissenting church with its lancet windows and twin towers. Nearly 50 years later, the congregation moved to a new building in Northumberland Road and the New Bridge Street church was sold to the Dominicans and re-erected at Byker (minus one tower) as St Lawrence's Roman Catholic Church. Offices now occupy the New Bridge Street site.

52 Church of the Divine Unity, New Bridge Street
Again, unusually for a nonconformist church, the exterior was designed by John Dobson in an elaborate style, though the interior plan was more conventional. It opened in 1854 for the congregation that moved from Hanover Square and could seat up to 600. Demolished in 1880, along with Carliol Tower, it was replaced by the new Free Library, which opened a year later.

53 Carliol Tower, New Bridge Street
Another of the medieval towers that once formed part of Newcastle's Town Wall, it was probably financed by the well-known and wealthy Carliol family, who lived nearby in Pilgrim Street. Later it became known as the Weavers' Tower because for many years, from the late 17th century, it was the headquarters of that guild.

54 John Dobson's House, New Bridge Street
John Dobson designed this classical-style stone villa for himself in 1823 and lived here for over 40 years until his death in 1865. His daughter lived here for another 40 years. It later became a cheap boarding house and then, for many years, it formed part of the Oxford Galleries Ballroom. A night club now occupies the building.

Just round the corner from John Dobson's House is Higham Place. In 1819 William Batson of Higham Dykes near Ponteland, a corn merchant, banker and alderman, commissioned the young Richard Grainger to build a terrace of substantial three-storey brick houses. So anxious was Grainger to succeed in his first important contract that he worked from 3am to 9pm each day. Only three of the original houses remain, all commercially occupied.

55 Baptist Chapel, New Bridge Street
Opened in 1839, at the south west end of the New Bridge, by a breakaway group of Baptists, it consisted of a chapel to seat 227, built over two storeys of dwellings on the bankside of Pandon Dene. The Central Motorway now covers the site.

56 Lying-in Hospital, New Bridge Street
Pregnant women would normally expect to give birth at home, with an attending midwife and doctor, but for those too poor to afford even the most basic medical care, this hospital opened in 1826 with facilities for seven patients. John Dobson, who lived opposite, drew up his plans free of charge. There were strict conditions of entry which included the need to have a fixed address and a marriage certificate, be free from disease and be able to provide clothing for the baby. The premises were taken over by the BBC in 1925 and are used today as offices.

The Church of the Divine Unity, New Bridge Street, in the 1850s. Carliol Tower and the chimneys of Higham Place are on the right. Trinity Presbyterian Church is far left.

57 Trafalgar Street
Opened around the 1820s, it has now all but disappeared owing to the construction of the Central Motorway in the late 1960s.

58 Manors Goods Station, Trafalgar Street
Designed by John Dobson on a landfill site over the former Pandon Dene, this spacious single-storey stone building opened in 1849 for use by the York, Newcastle and Berwick

Railway. Demolished nearly 60 years later, the site is today covered by the Central Business and Technology Park.

59 Oxford Street

Developed in the early 1800s as a residential thoroughfare, it too fell victim in the late 1960s to the Central Motorway.

60 Saville Row, Saville Place and Ellison Place

Described as 'a retired and elegant street' these substantial three-storey brick houses catered for some of the better-off townspeople who were anxious to leave the increasingly industrialised Quayside area in about 1770. It was named after Sir George Saville, a popular local figure, who lived here 1776-77. He was colonel of the First Battalion of the West York Militia. The former houses are now commercially occupied and the thoroughfare pedestrianised.

Just east of Saville Row is Saville Place. Many of these three-storey brick houses in terrace format, built around 1810 and described shortly afterwards as 'a range of good houses', were demolished in the 1960s for the construction of John Dobson Street.

East of Saville Place is Ellison Place. These top-of-the-range three-storey brick terraced houses were named after the local long-established Ellison family of merchants, clergymen and politicians upon whose land they were built. Dating from

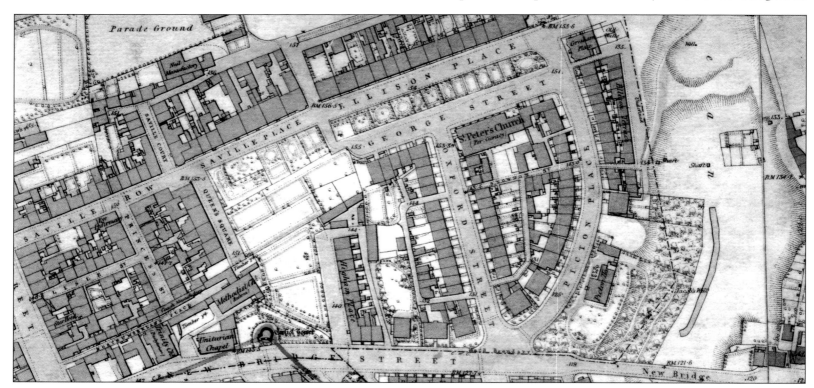

The OS map (1858-1865) shows the vanished streets of this area.

around 1810, they had generous gardens and shrubberies at the front, together with good views of the cricket field at the rear and were described as 'the genteelest and best built part of town', being 'retired, lofty and airy'. Newcastle's Mansion House occupied one as these houses for over 60 years, but now the whole terrace forms part of Northumbria University.

South of Saville Row, Princess Street consisted of 'a number of commodious houses', built around 1820 and removed in the late 1960s to make way for the old Central Library. Queens Square, also built in about 1820, a 'row of handsome houses' overlooking gardens, was replaced by John Dobson Street at the same time.

61 Public Baths, Bath Road (later Northumberland Road)
Opened in 1839, conveniently close to the Pandon Burn, they replaced earlier public baths at Bath Lane. Designed by John Dobson, this stone building had an impressive main entrance with piazza and consisted of a plunge pool (104ft long by 52ft wide and up to five feet deep) surrounded by over 50 small rooms used as either bathrooms or dressing rooms – men on the north side and women to the south. These rooms varied in size and the bathrooms contained different types of

The old Northumberland Road Baths from the 1928 souvenir programme of the opening of the new baths.

baths (warm, tepid, shower, vapour or rain) with some having fire places and WCs. A plunge or a shower bath each cost sixpence, a warm bath was a shilling and vapour baths 1s 6d. The baths were underused, largely due to an irregular supply of water and undersized storage cisterns. To counter a loss of income, the east side of the building facing the cricket field became the players' club house and another part was converted into an inn. The site was cleared in 1925 and superseded by the present City Baths and City Hall three years later.

62 Riding School, Bath Road (later Northumberland Road)
Designed by John Dobson for the Northumberland Yeomanry, this brick building opened in 1847. Today it forms part of Northumbria University.

63 St Thomas's School, Vine Lane
Opened in 1838 by Richard Clayton, Chaplain of nearby St Thomas's Chapel, this two-storey stone building accommodated 150 boys on the ground floor and 130 girls on the floor above, with separate entrances. The staff at this time consisted of a master and mistress, five pupil teachers, two assistants and seven monitors, the fees were a penny per week for reading and twopence for reading writing and arithmetic. The school closed in the 1930s, since when various uses have been made of the premises. Vine Lane got its name from the Vine Inn which once traded here.

64 Manors Police Station and Magistrates Court
Designed by John Dobson, the Court moved here from the Guildhall in 1836. Magistrates attended daily on the first floor. There were five prison cells (with a WC attached to each one!) on the ground floor. The Police Station and Court moved to Pilgrim Street in 1874.

8 All Saints Church to Pandon

1 Pilgrim Street

One of the routes through the town to and from the medieval bridge, it was used by people travelling on pilgrimages between religious establishments. It became a commercial backwater after the opening of the High Level Bridge in 1849 but revived nearly 80 years later following the completion of the New Tyne Bridge in 1928.

2 All Saints Church, Pilgrim Street

To celebrate the opening of this splendid new Georgian Church in 1796, a soldier in the Cheshire militia, John Burdikin, performed a handstand at the top of the steeple, 195 feet above ground level, on a stone less than three feet in diameter. He remained upside down 'for some time'. All Saints Church replaced the medieval All Hallows Church, almost on the same site. The oval design meant everyone could now see the altar, the acoustics were excellent, and it could hold up to 2,000 worshippers. David Stephenson, Newcastle's leading architect at this time, designed the building and lies buried in the churchyard. The church was deconsecrated in 1961 but reopened 35 years later, not as a parish church, but as Saint Willibrord with All Saints Anglican Catholic Church.

3 Silver Street

At one time known as Jew-Gate, because it is thought Jewish dealers in silver plate lived there. Other names have included All-Hallow-Gate and Temple-Gate. Modern apartments and an office block occupy one side of the street opposite All Saints churchyard.

Silver Street, from All Saints churchyard, 1885.

4 Dog Bank

Its exact derivation is unknown but in earlier times it had also been called Silver Street (silver dealers lived here too), when the other Silver Street (above)was known as All-Hallow-Gate. The old buildings have been replaced by modern town houses.

5 Manor Chare

Led from the King's Manor, formerly the Augustinian Friary and now the Holy Jesus Hospital, down to Cowgate. Today the street has been realigned parallel with the rail viaduct and no longer passes beneath the viaduct at the original arch.

Railway Bridge over Manor Chare

Built in 1847-48 (architect unknown) to carry the Newcastle and Berwick Railway to the Central Station (1850), and from

there to the planned High Level Bridge. It continues to carry the main East Coast railway.

6 Stockbridge (at foot of Manor Chare and Silver Street)

Originally the site of a wooden bridge (stock means wood) at the junction of the Pandon and Erick Burns. A fish market was held in this area 'where boats came up from the river'. An adjoining street was called Fishergate. Modern developments have transformed the area.

7 Cowgate (between the foot of Silver Street and Dog Bank)

Before the creation of Dean Street and Mosley Street in the 1780s this was an alternative route to the quayside and bridge for cattle and carriages, because it was less steep and dangerous. Modern developments now cover one side of this short street.

8 Broad Chare

First mentioned in the late 14th century, following extensive land reclamation from the river, it became the widest of Newcastle's 20 Chares and just 'broad enough to admit a cart'. Today it is a much wider thoroughfare, part of which has been pedestrianised.

9 Trinity House, Broad Chare

In 1505 a collection of buildings was erected around a courtyard on this new site for the Guild or Fraternity of the Blessed Trinity of Newcastle upon Tyne. These buildings included meeting rooms, a chapel and almshouses for the brethren. When it moved into the buildings the Guild changed its name to the 'Society of Masters and Mariners'. Their purpose was to look after the safety and welfare of seafarers, the river and the coastline between Holy Island and Whitby with particular reference to beacons, buoys, lighthouses and pilotage. None of the original buildings have survived in their entirety, most have been rebuilt and others added, including a school where Cuthbert Collingwood and James Cook received some of their education. Trinity House continues to function, albeit on a reduced scale.

10 Queen Street, Lombard Street, King Street

Much of the medieval property in this area had been destroyed during the Great Fire of 1854. John Dobson then produced an ambitious scheme to rebuild the area and link it to the upper parts of Newcastle. These Quayside streets and buildings were largely completed 1858-63 by various architects but the links with the upper town never came to pass. Many of the new buildings were offices connected to the booming shipping trade but are now mostly shops and restaurants.

11 Exchange Buildings, Quayside

Framed by Queen Street, Lombard Street and King Street on land devastated in 1854 by the Great Fire, it opened in 1861/2 as 'palatial mercantile offices' for local coal shipping and associated businesses. Today a restaurant and hotel occupy the premises.

12 Tyne-Tees Shipping Company Offices, King Street

Dating from 1875 (seemingly too late for Storey's picture, though he may have had access to plans), it was designed in a mix of Elizabethan and Jacobean styles. It retains a destination board on an outside wall, advertising passenger liner services. A restaurant now occupies the building.

13 Cail's Buildings, Quayside

Septimus Cail, one of ten children, began his working life in these premises working with his brother John as opticians and nautical instrument makers. He later started a printing and stationery business on the same site, which was continued by his sons for many years. A modern office block, with shops at ground level, now occupies the site.

14 Customs House, Quayside
Dating from 1766, it was refronted by Sidney Smirke (John Dobson's son-in-law) nearly 40 years later and fortunately survived the Great Fire of 1854. The collection of customs duties on the Tyne is said to have begun due to the import of large quantities of wine in the 13th century. Barristers' offices now occupy the building.

Trinity Chare is just to the right of the Customs House. It is one of Newcastle's 20 or so chares (narrow alleys), and leads to the rear of Trinity House from the Quayside. In the 1860s it contained 11 businesses including a ship owner, ship brokers, coal exporters and a bonded whisky warehouse. Today the chare is merely an uninhabited alternative route to Trinity House.

15 Kettle's Store, Quayside
The site of this former 'outfitter and clothier' owned by James Kettle, on the corner of Spicer Chare and the Quayside, is now covered by the Law Courts.

16 Bonded Warehouses, Cock's Chare and Love Lane
These tall, mainly brick, bonded warehouses were purpose-built 1801-1830 to fit into the existing network of chares. Some of the lower walls are of stone, which is said to have

The Quayside around 1895. More than 30 years after John Storey produced his panorama nothing much has changed. Compare this photograph to the picture. You can just make out Wall Knoll Tower (see page 69) in the distance. Behind the Tower is St Cuthbert's Church, a later structure.

come from the demolition of the nearby Town Wall. Today the warehouses have been successfully converted or rebuilt (following a major fire) into luxury apartments.

The narrow alley on the left of the shaded warehouse is Cock's Chare (now Cox Chare). Ralph Cock, a wealthy 17th century merchant, alderman and mayor once lived here. Four of his daughters (out of 15 children) gave rise to an old local saying 'as rich as Cock's canny hinnies'; they apparently all married 'most eligible husbands'. The Law Courts now occupy one side of the chare with apartments on the other.

On the right of the shaded warehouse is Love Lane, the birthplace, in 1751, of John Scott (husband of Bessie Surtees) later to become Lord Eldon. Scott's substantial home was replaced around 1830 by bonded warehouses. During the 1860s occupants included a chemical manufacturer, corn merchants, ship brokers and a beer seller.

17 Hydraulic Crane, Quayside

In 1845 William George Armstrong, a qualified solicitor, suggested to Newcastle Council the economic advantages of converting existing cranes on Newcastle's quayside to hydraulic power. From a young age Armstrong had been fascinated by hydraulics, yet he had never had any formal engineering training. The Council was satisfied with his initial conversion, so much so that Armstrong and four others formed the Newcastle Cranage Company two years later on a greenfield site at Elswick. It became the forerunner of a huge industrial organisation that was to diversify into armaments and shipbuilding. Here the crane seems to be lifting a large, heavy boiler into or out of a steam collier. A hydraulic crane built by Armstrong-Mitchell in 1883 can still be seen in the Venice Arsenale.

18 Roman Catholic chapel, Wall Knoll

First opened in 1765, to accommodate 504 Presbyterian worshippers. Friction within the chapel prompted some members to move to New Bridge Street where the Trinity Presbyterian Church opened in 1847. It is not known when the Wall Knoll building became a Roman Catholic chapel. The construction of City Road in the early 1880s completely destroyed the Wall Knoll area.

19 Bethel Chapel, Forster Street

This small and convenient place of worship seating 159, dates from the early 1700s and was first used by the Glassite sect who had broken away from the Church of Scotland. Their founder, John Glass, had been expelled from the Church of Scotland in 1728. Sometimes members of this sect

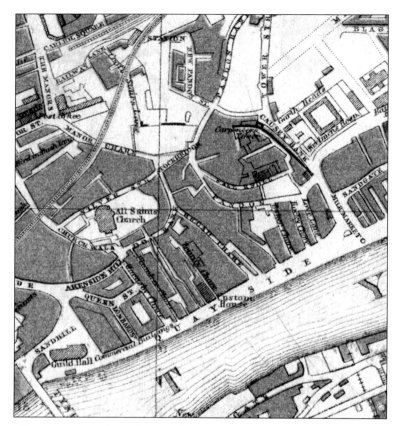

Christie's New Plan of 1865 shows the general layout of this part of the Quayside.

were described as Sandemanians after a later and enthusiastic follower called Robert Sandeman. Their ministers came from the town's tradesmen and 'avoided games of chance but accepted harmless amusements'. The Glassites worshiped here for 70 years. It is not known when it became a Bethel Chapel. Forster Street exists today, leading off Milk Market, amidst modern developments.

20 Sallyport Gate, Wall Knoll Tower

Now the only surviving gate in the medieval Town Wall, it was originally a minor gateway through which defenders could pass quietly to patrol the area outside. Rebuilt in 1716 by the Guild of Shipwrights as their headquarters, it later served as a school, furniture store and is now used for social functions.

21 Railway Bridge over Trafalgar Street

Designed in 1839 by John and Benjamin Green to connect the new Newcastle to North Shields Railway with its terminus at Carliol Square, Newcastle.

22 Lower Pandon Dene

This was the last part of the Pandon Burn to be infilled. Work began in around 1880 to realign the 18th century New Road. It became City Road in 1883. Much of the infill material came from the reduction in height of the Wall Knoll district. By 1886 the Pandon Burn had been fully culverted.

23 Pandon Bank

This sloping street alongside the Pandon Burn, connected the Pandon area with Shieldfield and originally passed through the Town Wall at the Pandon Gate (demolished). In 1736, a local historian wrote 'this way was within these four years the pleasantest entrance into Newcastle having gardens on each side beset with trees so large a size and shade that they covered the street itself in several places'. Today, part of Pandon Bank remains a busy thoroughfare but the lower section no longer exists, due to the creation of City Road in the early 1880s.

Pandon Bank and Pandon House around 1897.

24 Pandon House, Pandon Bank

Once the home of George Tallentire Gibson, who was a solicitor and owner of substantial property in the east end of Newcastle. The house eventually became a home for destitute boys for many years before demolition in the late 1920s. Luxury apartments now occupy the site.

25 Corn Warehouse, Pandon Bank

Opened in 1849 for the York, Newcastle and Berwick Railway, this multi-storey grain loft was designed by Benjamin Green. Severely damaged by bombing in 1941, its ground floor shell survived until the 1970s and the site continues to remain derelict.

9 Great North Road to the Ouseburn

1 St James' Place
This group of dwellings was built in the 1790s on the site of the former St James' Chapel and Leper Hospital. The Hancock Museum replaced these houses in 1878.

2 Great North Road
An ancient road, once the major east coast route between London and Scotland, now largely bypassed.

3 Chapel of St Andrew's Cemetery
One of a pair of chapels in this Municipal Cemetery which opened in 1858.

4 Northern Counties Deaf and Dumb Institution
This charitable organisation moved from Wellington Place (off Pilgrim Street) to this 6.5 acre site in 1861. It was considerably enlarged in 1905. Today the buildings contain the Northern Counties School and College.

5 Brandling Village
Named after the well-known local family of landowners, businessmen and public figures. Jesmond had been a farming and coal mining area, but the creation of the village probably marked its transition into the residential suburb that it is today. By the late 1820s 'about 100 convenient freehold houses and cottages' close to the Great North Road had been built to provide one of 'the pleasure abodes of the affluent' with a 'healthy and desirable country air' compared to the polluted atmosphere of the town centre. In the middle of the village there was a Wesleyan Chapel (1827) which was converted into a laundry in the 1890s and continued for a

Terraced housing in Brandling Village around 1912.

further 60 years. Most of the cottages were condemned and demolished in the 1930s.

6 Cemetery Road
Planned by John Dobson in the 1830s, it led to the cemetery he designed which opened in 1836 (see page 76). It was renamed Jesmond Road at a later date.

7 Carlton Terrace, Cemetery Road
These three-storey brick houses, now occupied by Newcastle University, were built in around 1840 to the design of John Dobson. The houses on the south side of the road, now restored, may be of a slightly later date.

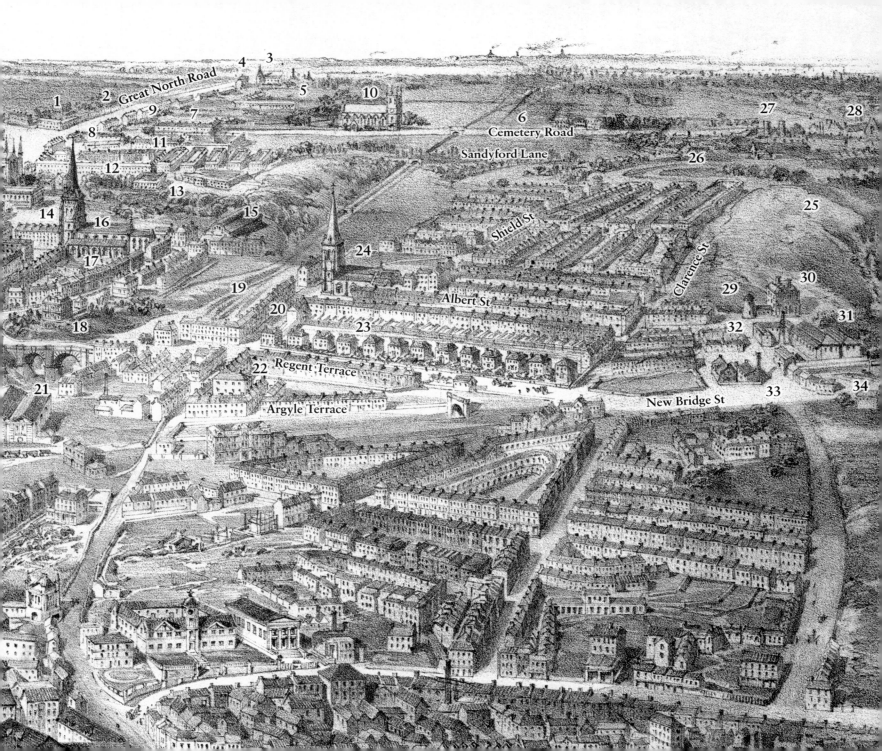

Great North Road

Cemetery Road

Sandyford Lane

Shield St

Clarence St

Albert St

Regent Terrace

Argyle Terrace

New Bridge St

8 St Mary's Terrace, Great North Road

Albany and John Hancock, the renowned naturalists, after whom the Natural History Museum is named, lived at No 4 for over 50 years until John's death in 1890. The premises are now used for commercial purposes.

9 Jesmond High Terrace, Great North Road

Charles Mark Palmer, the well-known Tyneside shipbuilder, businessman and politician resided for most of his life at No 1, though he also had homes in London and North Yorkshire. Newcastle University's Robinson Library now covers the site.

10 Jesmond Parish Church, Cemetery Road

This, the first parish church in the new and rapidly growing suburb of Jesmond, 'midst green fields and meadows', was consecrated in 1861. Designed by John Dobson and built in the Decorated style, it held 1,300 worshippers. The planned spire was never built because of lack of funds. The construction was financed largely by a breakaway group from St Thomas's Church, Barras Bridge, who became furious following the appointment of a 'High Church' vicar to replace their 'Evangelical' long-serving chaplain, the Reverend Richard Clayton, who died in 1856. Jesmond Parish Church acquired the attractive nickname of 'St Spite' from those who opposed its construction.

11 Vanished streets

The following thoroughfares: Nixon Street (1844), Simpson

Lovaine Crescent and the edge of the Pandon Dene, in around 1896.

Street (1850), Race Street (1853), initially York Street and then Hood Street, Day Street (1855), Alma Street (1857), Marianople Street (1857) in this part of Sandyford no longer exist and the area is now dominated by the Civic Centre and Northumbria University. The streets were named after local landowners, businessmen or a contemporary event. The Malt Kilns on Sandyford Lane belonged to Addison Potter, a brewer of Heaton Hall, and were later superseded by the purpose-built Burton Brewery.

12 Lovaine Place

Described as 'being in one of the sweetest situations in the vicinity of the town', these substantial three-storey houses were built in the early 1820s. 'Lovaine' is probably derived from 'Louvain' and may have French connections with the local aristocratic Percy family.

13 Lovaine Terrace (1844), Lovaine Crescent (1850), and the rim of Pandon Dene

Pandon Dene, 'A romantic place full of hills and vales with a picturesque old mill and ancient water wheel', is how this section of the Pandon Burn appeared in early Victorian times. The burn rose near Spital Tongues and flowed into the Tyne near the present-day Law Courts. Culverting of the burn was completed in the 1880s.

14 Cricket Ground, Bath Road (now Northumberland Road)

Cricket matches were held on the Town Moor until 1839 when they were transferred to this open area, formerly Great Magdalene Close. It became the home of the Northumberland Cricket Club for more than 40 years. Most games were played during the week, rarely at weekends, and there was musical entertainment during intervals.

In 1859 a gala evening took place, the highlight of which

The Cricket Club, 1853, with the Baths in use as a club house. St Thomas's School (see page 63) is between the club house and St Thomas's Church.

was to be a balloon ascent by a gymnast. To everyone's amazement he performed on a trapeze at 1,000 feet, shortly after which the balloon became erratic and eventually drifted out of sight. Apparently the balloon neared the ground across the Tyne at Felling and while attempting to escape, the gymnast tragically fell 120 feet. He died three days later at the Infirmary. The balloon was never recovered.

The cricket field was required for developments in 1881 and the Northumberland County Cricket Club moved to Heaton Lane (now Heaton Road) for 17 years before moving to the present ground at Osborne Avenue, Jesmond.

15 A mystery building

It has been impossible to determine the identity of this structure, however an 1879 directory includes a reference to a building in this area serving as a Drill Hall and HQ for the 1st Newcastle Engineer Volunteers. This date is somewhat late for the picture but the hall may have been in existence for some years beforehand and not recorded. It is worth noting there had been a Parade Ground in nearby Bath Road, adjacent to the Riding School, from an early date.

16 St Peter's Church, Ellison Place

Consecrated in 1843, it was initially a Chapel of Ease to St Andrew's Parish Church in Newgate Street. Designed by John Dobson in the Decorated style to seat over 1,100 worshippers, it eventually became a parish church. Demolished in 1936, some of its materials and furnishings were recycled to extend the Church of St Michael with St Lawrence at Byker. The Church of the Divine Unity has stood on the site since 1940.

17 Picton Place

Dating from the 1820s and overlooking Pandon Dene, 'it contained the best of John Dobson's classical urban villas'.

Demolished early in the 20th century for railway developments, the site has now been covered by the Central Motorway.

18 Picton House, Picton Place
A substantial classical villa overlooking Pandon Dene, designed by John Dobson in around 1825. In 1864 it became the terminus and ticket office of the Blyth and Tyne Railway. It later served as a coal depot, then as an Employment Exchange before being demolished to make way for the New Bridge Street roundabout.

19 Blyth and Tyne Rail Terminus
A projected increase in passenger rail traffic between Newcastle and Tynemouth resulted in an extension of the rail network in 1864. It involved a track (with stations) through Gosforth and Jesmond which made use of the now infilled Pandon Dene for a short distance north of this terminus. Forty five years later the terminus was moved 300 yards further south to link up with the main East Coast line at a new station called Manors North. Modern developments have superseded both of these termini.

20 Pleasant Row
These three-storey brick plain fronted houses (with attics) plus gardens at the rear stretching down to the Pandon Dene, were built in around 1800. Lord Armstrong, the Tyneside industrialist, was born at No 9 and the stone door

King Charles' House is on the left, and Shieldfield Green just to the right in this 1890 photograph.

lintel 'Armstrong House' is preserved in a nearby stone wall. Railway expansion in 1901 caused its demolition.

21 New Bridge
Designed by John Stokoe, this elegant triple-arched bridge opened in 1812. It disappeared in 1886 following the culverting of the Pandon Burn and the infilling of the Dene.

22 Caledonian Chapel, Argyle Street
Closing in 1892, after 51 years as a Church of Scotland Chapel, it ended its life as a warehouse for a prominent local firm of seed merchants in the 1960s.

23 Ridley Villas, New Bridge Street
Popular with local businessmen, these 24 semi-detached homes were built in the 1820s on land owned by Sir Matthew White Ridley. They each had neat front gardens with good kitchen gardens behind. Most of the premises are now commercially occupied.

24 Shieldfield Green
Inhabited at least from the 17th century, this triangular area of land has remained largely undeveloped. In 1801 it was regarded as 'a most pleasant and airy retreat for men of business of any in the vicinity; the houses command a most extensive and entertaining prospect and have beautiful gardens adjoining Pandon Dene.'

Christ Church, Shieldfield Green
Built as an additional parish church in the expanding and crowded parish of

Pandon Dene from the north, with the New Bridge (1812) in the background, around 1821.

All Saints over part of what had been the 17th century Shieldfield fort. Consecrated in 1861, it was designed by A.B. Higham in the Decorated Gothic style to seat 500. Initially there was a two-year waiting list to join the congregation.

King Charles' House, Shieldfield Green
During his imprisonment at Newcastle in 1646-47, King Charles I reputedly rested here during games of goff (golf) nearby. Demolished about 1961, a multi-storey block of flats (King Charles Tower) now stands close by.

It took about 40 years for Shieldfield to develop fully as a residential suburb. When completed in the 1870s it had a population of nearly 13,000. The Victorian two-storey brick terraced houses have now been replaced with modern terraced housing and a few tower blocks of apartments. Shieldfield streets completed by the mid 1860s included: Shield Street, Wesley Street, Carlton Street, Canada Street, Clarence Street, Gosforth Street, Copland Terrace, Albert Street and Sandyford Lane, renamed Sandyford Road in 1878.

25 Sandyford Dene
Also known as Dropping Well Ravine or Rosedale, the Sandyford Burn rose on the Town Moor and flowed down through Jesmond, to the Ouseburn here. Now culverted and infilled, the section near Sandyford Lane was the scene of Lambert's Leap in 1759.

26 Lambert's Leap, Sandyford Lane
The scene of a dramatic accident in 1759, when a 16-year-old rider, Cuthbert Lambert, failed to negotiate the awkward approach to the bridge over Sandyford Dene

Jesmond Road around 1912. Jesmond Old Cemetery is on the left, and All Saints Cemetery on the right.

(now infilled). Lambert's horse was killed and he only survived by clinging to an overhanging tree. A commemorative stone is included in a low brick wall near the scene.

27 Jesmond Old Cemetery, Cemetery Road
The last resting place of many of Tyneside's better known personalities, it opened as a private cemetery in 1836 as an alternative to the overcrowded and unhealthy parish churchyards of the time. Well-known people buried here include John Dobson, the cemetery's architect and department store founders Emerson Muschamp Bainbridge and John James Fenwick.

28 All Saints Cemetery, Cemetery Road
Opened in 1857 as a municipal cemetery, in response to the national closure of urban parish churchyards two years earlier because of the cholera epidemic. The architect was Benjamin Green.

29 Union Windmill, Union Terrace

The earliest reference is 1827, when it is described as a corn mill. However by 1860, it is mapped as a ruin and today the site is covered by a small industrial estate off Stoddart Street.

30 The Biscuit Factory, Stoddart Street

Built by the late 1860s, it was run by Thomas Squire & Sons until just before First World War. Thereafter, for over 30 years, the Edinburgh brewers T. Usher and Son Ltd occupied the building. After spells as a general warehouse and a major conversion, it is now Europe's largest commercial art gallery (opened in 2004).

31 Waterproof Cover Factory, Union Terrace

Built in 1857, to serve the North Eastern Railway (a railtrack ran into the factory), it operated for over a century at this address. Today the site is vacant, awaiting re-development with only some of its lower stone walls visible.

32 Woollen Flock Factory, Union Terrace

Again, probably dating from the mid 1850s, nothing is known of its later history. The site is derelict at the moment with only its lower stone wall visible and awaits re-development.

33 Sawmill, Stepney

Almost certainly belonging to the timber merchants, Hardy Brothers, and conveniently close to the Stepney Tannery and railway.

A detail from The Ouseburn Viaduct painted by J.W. Carmichael, 1839. Stepney Windmill is on the right. The Lead Works are in the middle distance alongside the Ouseburn.

34 Ouseburn Rail Viaduct

Opened in 1839 to the design of celebrated local architects, John and Benjamin Green, it formed part of the new Newcastle and North Shields railway. The arches of the viaduct were initially made of laminated timber, for cheapness, but were replaced (with wrought iron) 30 years later. It remained a pedestrian toll bridge (the toll was a halfpenny) for nearly 50 years, after which the viaduct was doubled in width to cope with the increased volume of traffic on the East Coast main line.

10 New Bridge Street to the Tyne

1 Tower Street
Named after the adjacent Wall Knoll Tower on the Town Wall which contained the Sallyport Gate. The Roman Wall (Hadrian's Wall) is thought to have passed over Wall Knoll on its way to Wallsend. Tower Street is now bisected by the more recent Melbourne Street.

2 Causey Bank
Originally connected Milk Market with Tower Street. 'Causey' is thought to derive from the French word 'caucie' meaning an embankment or raised way (as in 'causeway'). Little remains of the original thoroughfare due to the construction of City Road (19th century) and the Quayside Highway (20th century).

3 Wilkinson's Buildings and Conduit Head
Consisted of some 'neat and beautiful' 18th century houses, once the property of Thomas Wilkinson, a successful joiner and cabinet maker. They formed part of a square of buildings in this elevated part of town. The area was also known as Conduit Head and was reputedly one of the town's earliest sources of water, because of its 'many fine springs'. There was a cistern in one of the gardens from where water was conveyed in lead pipes (conduits) to various pants (public fountains) in the lower parts of town. Modern developments now cover the area.

4 Stepney Lane
An 18th century thoroughfare that linked Pandon Bank to the Stepney windmill area. Nothing remains of the original houses and industrial buildings.

5 Unidentified building
This may have been occupied by T.C. Hardy & Co. (Timber Merchant) whose saw mills were also in Stepney Lane. Modern developments now cover the site.

6 New Road
Initially laid out in 1776 to connect Milk Market with North Shields, it was re-aligned at a higher level about a century later and extended to Pilgrim Street following the infilling of lower Pandon Dene. It was renamed City Road in 1883 in response to Newcastle's elevation to city status.

7 Keelmen's Hospital, New Road
It is said charity begins at home and the building of this hospital was probably the first local example. A visiting bishop remarked, shortly after its completion in 1701, that he had 'seen many hospitals, the works of rich men but it was

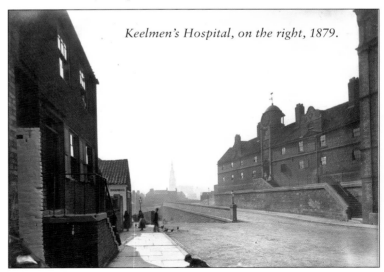

Keelmen's Hospital, on the right, 1879.

5

Stepney Lane 4

3

14

15   16

30

Tower Street

1

Gibson Street

18

Elwick's Lane

7

8

9

13

10   6

17

11

12   New Road

19

Causey Bank

2

Sandgate

20

28

21

Milk Market

22

23

24   27

25   26   29

the first he ever saw or heard of which had been built by the poor'. A keelman's life as a Tyne barge man was harsh and very physical with most of them being unfit to carry on beyond the age of 40. They agreed to contribute fourpence per tide towards the construction of a hospital or almshouse 'for poor keelmen and keelmen's widows'. This two-storey brick structure originally consisted of 60 small rooms around a grass courtyard, initially at an annual rent of a shilling per room. Today it accommodates university students in enlarged rooms.

8 Royal Jubilee School, New Road

This first major building designed by John Dobson opened in 1810 (the 50th anniversary of King George III's accession to the throne) to teach children of the poor reading, writing, spelling and arithmetic, with a minimum requirement that every such child could at least read the Bible. The school became one of Tyneside's 'must visit' places for distinguished visitors because of its novel teaching methods which included the monitorial system and also lessons given in rhyme. 'It is a curious and pleasing spectacle to see above 400 boys [roughly the school's capacity] in one room, actively and cheerfully engaged in acquiring the elements of education'. Annual subscribers were entitled to recommend suitable pupils at the rate of half a guinea per boy. A similar school for girls was established four years later at Croft Street, off New Bridge Street. A Salvation Army Men's Hostel opened on the site around 1976.

9 Ragged and Industrial School, New Road

Another building by John Dobson, it opened in 1854, paid for by a small group of philanthropists. Eventually, about 250 boys and girls attended in roughly equal numbers. Nearly one third were lodged and clothed by the school. Subjects

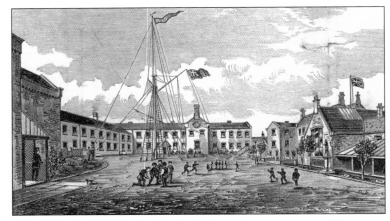

The Ragged and Industrial School from the west. The buildings shown seem to fit in with Storey's picture, though they are not evident on the 1858-1865 OS map.

taught included, for boys, printing, tailoring, making sacks, mats and other practical skills. Girls learned to make clothes and the duties of domestic servants. Discipline does not seem to have been a problem, corporal punishment being virtually unknown as a stern look or an appropriate word was enough. The site is now occupied by the Salvation Army Men's Hostel.

10 Public Baths and Wash-houses, New Road

Provided by the Town Corporation in 1848, these were Newcastle's first public baths and wash-houses. They were superseded in 1906 by a new building at the corner of New Bridge Street and Gibson Street, which still exists although not for its original purpose. The Salvation Army Men's Hostel now covers the site.

11 Methodist Chapel, New Road

John Dobson designed this substantial Wesleyan Chapel to hold 1600 people. It opened in 1813. Pews were rent free to encourage 'the religious poor of Sandgate'. Initially, to generate income, the chapel basement was sub-let as a bonded warehouse. Later in the 19th century the chapel became a brewery, then a marine store, and after a period as a Salvation Army Hostel, it finally became part of Hedley's Soap Works. The Quayside Highway has obliterated the site.

12 Hedley's Soap Works, New Road

John Greene's tallow chandler's business moved here from Gateshead in 1838, primarily to satisfy the huge demand for candles (made from hard tallow). At this time, soap (made from soft tallow) was merely a byproduct. Thomas Hedley spent over 50 years working here, first of all as a manager and then as proprietor of this successful business. It received a massive boost in 1853 following the scrapping of tax on tallow as a result of the cholera outbreak of that year (soap being a much-needed commodity). Procter and Gamble took over the business in 1930 and today the Sandgate car park and Quayside Highway occupy the site.

The OS 1858-1865 map shows the whole area including the gas works. The narrow alleys behind Sandgate were overcrowded and disease-ridden.

13 Gibson Street

Named after the prominent Newcastle solicitor, George Tallentire Gibson, one of the town's largest property owners. He engaged Thomas Oliver, one of Newcastle's most talented architects, to plan streets in this area, 'with neat two- and three-storey houses suited to the wants of the humble, yet respectable, classes of the community'.

The district became known as Gibson Town and was completed between 1836 and 1848. Gibson was also instrumental in the redevelopment of the Quayside following the Great Fire of 1854, and at one time had been in favour of converting the Lower Ouseburn valley into a dock. His work and development schemes meant long hours at his office in St Nicholas Square and on at least two occasions he was subjected to violent assault during his walk home to Pandon House late at night. Susanna, his widow and cousin who survived him by over 20 years, continued to support his developments and it is probable the New Road re-alignment (to become City Road) would not have proceeded without her generosity. The Gibsons were also benevolent to charities and Pandon House, their family home, was finally donated as a shelter for destitute boys (see page 69). Both Susanna and George, staunch Methodists, are buried in the non-conformist cemetery at Westgate Hill.

Other streets built as part of Gibson Town included Melbourne Street, Buxton Street (containing Buxton Street Methodist Chapel), Upper Buxton Street, Blagdon Street, Richmond Street and Howard Street.

14 Victoria Bazaar

As an integral part of the Gibson Town development, it opened in 1838 on a triangular site as a shopping arcade for the sale of meat and vegetables. Designed by Thomas Oliver,

The buildings of Victoria Bazaar in 1957.

it consisted of two storeys 'with forty-two shops at ground level and offices above, reached from a gallery on pillars suggestive of a corner in some continental town'. Soon, unable to compete with Richard Grainger's larger indoor market in central Newcastle, opened three years earlier, it was converted into dwellings. Following an abortive attempt to re-site Newcastle's Green Market here in 1962 (it moved to Gateshead's Team Valley Trading Estate) Gibson Town was gradually demolished. Student accommodation has now replaced the Bazaar.

15 Red Barns

Little is known about this small group of buildings that appear on the first detailed map of Newcastle dated 1723. The 'fairly large and ugly' building was probably a farmhouse together with some 'terraced housing' amid fields. In 1863 the site was taken over by the Dominicans and ten years later their fine Gothic church, designed by A.M. Dunn, opened to cater for an increasing number of Roman Catholic residents. The adjoining Priory opened in 1887.

16 Stepney Windmill (see page 77)

It is said that no other UK town had so many windmills as Newcastle and its suburbs. In 1825 there were 49. Most windmills ground corn, but this one was probably also grinding bark (from nearby timber yards) for an adjacent tannery. It first appears in records in 1698. A severe storm in 1839 tore off the wands and shortly afterwards the Tanners Arms pub opened next to the stone tower of the former mill.

17 Egypt

In 1796 Britain was under the threat of naval blockade and invasion. It is said that timber sheds near this site were built to store grain in troubled times. According to the Bible story, Egypt was where grain could be obtained in times of famine. This is probably why the name Egypt was adopted for Newcastle's emergency grain store. The original timber storage sheds, briefly used as army barracks in 1803, have now been replaced by permanent buildings including a pub.

18 Elwick's (Ellick's) Lane (Lonnen)

Before the opening of the New Road in 1776, this thoroughfare was the route for carriages between Newcastle and Shields via Ouseburn Bridge. A reference exists to 'coals being carried from a pit in Shieldfield via Elwick's Lonnen and then down St Ann's Street to the shipping staith'. The name was changed to Crawhall Road in recognition of that family's ropery business nearby.

19 St Ann's Chapel School

Built in 1682, largely at the town's expense, and with the mayor as governor. About 100 children attended in the 1820s and for 1s 2d a month they would be taught reading, writing and arithmetic. It was possible to learn reading only for the bargain price of eightpence a month. A modern hotel now covers the site. St Ann's Church is off the picture to the right.

Sandgate around 1900.

20 Sandgate

A street as well as a district, it takes its name from the Sand Gate, one of the six principal gates on the medieval Town Wall. It probably refers to the once sandy shore alongside the Tyne before land reclamation took place. Sandgate was the most populous of all the town's suburbs – 'a vast number of narrow lanes crowded with houses and chiefly inhabited by people that worked upon the river particularly the keelmen. In 1854 about 5,000 people were crowded into 350 houses with only 'one public privy, three private privies and four private WCs to serve them'. Water was provided by just two pants, at Milkmarket and Swirle, that operated irregularly. This area, now changed utterly, has been rebuilt with offices, apartments and a hotel.

21 Sandgate pant (or street fountain)

This was one of 50 pants in Newcastle in around 1844. Twelve (including this one) were free of charge and funded by

Children at the Sandgate pant in around 1900.

the Corporation. The remainder were known as 'Farden' pants, and customers were charged by the water company provider at a farthing per five-gallon tub or 'skeel' for water from them. Pants typically consisted of a stone structure enclosing a lead-lined cistern with brass taps, fed from springs, wells or Water Company reservoirs. Most of these pants also incorporated a trough for the use of horses 'or for common domestic purposes'. The word 'pant' probably originated from the medieval word 'pand' (pond) which in turn came from the Anglo Saxon 'pyndan' meaning to enclose or shut up.

Until about 1770 townspeople obtained their water free of charge from the pants, but they were not without problems. Water was often only available on one or two days each week. Emergency measures had to be taken, which included halting the sinking of new coal pits or quarries

(nearby springs could be affected), stopping the water supply to the brewery, and restricting piped water to private subscribers unless they were town dignitaries (Mayor, Sheriff, Town Clerk, Recorder and Aldermen).

Later, as the population grew, as the fire risk increased, and as steam engines became available, water infrastructure appeared in the form of additional reservoirs, aqueducts, pumping stations, piping and more pants. Newcastle Corporation could no longer provide free water to all, and so charges were made at most new pants. However, there was still conflict. Not only were water shortages still common, but it became apparent that buying water by the skeel was more expensive than having it piped direct into your house at an annual cost of between 18 and 30 shillings.

Prompted by the cholera outbreaks of the 1830s and 1840s, developments began to take place which culminated with the formation of the Whittle Dean Water Company in 1845 and the Newcastle and Gateshead Water Company in 1863.

22 The 'Folly'

In an attempt to improve water supply in late 17th century Newcastle, Captain Cuthbert Dykes, the town surveyor, postmaster and hostman was sanctioned by the Corporation to erect a building to contain a steam-driven water engine to raise and filter water from the Tyne 'for the convenience of brew houses and victualling houses etc'. Completed in 1693, it did not operate for more than a few years because of disputed land ownership and doubts over contaminated water. Expensive litigation followed and Dykes was fined £2,000 after which the 'Folly', as it became known, was converted into a large grain warehouse. Modern developments now cover the site.

23 Milk Market

Situated just outside the Sand Gate (demolished 1798), it was first mentioned in 1717 when a market keeper was appointed. Large quantities of milk and other produce were sold here daily. The seasonal hiring of farm workers took place here too. In late Victorian times, the vicinity became known as Paddy's Market, 'where old clothes were laid on straw upon the street' for sale on Saturdays.

24 Leith Steam Packet Office

In 1824 a steamer named the *Newcastle* began a service between Newcastle and Leith.

STEAM COMMUNICATION

BETWEEN

NEWCASTLE, LEITH, AND EDINBURGH.

THE SPLENDID & POWERFUL NEW IRON PADDLE STEAMSHIP

"BRITANNIA,"

Or other Steamer, Sails between NEWCASTLE and LEITH TWICE A-WEEK, from each End throughout the Year, and makes the Passage in about NINE HOURS. Particulars of Sailing and Fares will be found in the *Newcastle Courant*, and in the different Local Papers; and for Freight, &c., apply at the Company's Offices in Leith, at 34, Bernard Street; in Edinburgh, at 20, Waterloo Place; in Glasgow, to Bankier, Lietke and Co., 25, Gordon Street; in Newcastle, at the Leith Steam Wharf, New Quay, to **DAVID DUNN, Agent.**

The Leith Steam packet Office advertises in 1871.

25 New Quay

The New Quay replaced the Low Way (which had been a narrow and congested street) in the early 1840s.

26 London Steam Packet Office

The first steam boat service between Newcastle and London began in 1824 with the *Rapid*. It took 56 hours.

27 Tyne Brewery, Sandgate

First mentioned in the late 18th century, it had its own riverside wharf and was one of several breweries in Newcastle and district. It moved to larger purpose-built buildings at Bath Lane in 1868.

28 Gas Works, Sandgate

Newcastle's third gas works opened here in 1833. The initial works had been at Forth Street (1817) followed by a larger replacement at Manors (1823). Not everyone had been happy about the change to gas lighting; shopkeepers feared they would lose customers and others felt disgruntled persons would simply move away from towns. Even Sir Humphry Davy, the eminent chemist, ridiculed the idea of lighting towns with gas and asked one of the planners 'if it was intended to take the dome of St Paul's for a gas holder'. Similarly Newcastle Town Council also had doubts, 'if the mayor chooses to use gas in the Mansion House, rather than oil or candles, let him pay for it'. The Sandgate and Manors works closed in 1859 to be replaced by larger gas works at Low Elswick. (For more on gas works see page 94.)

A cattle sanatorium (a quarantine to ensure animals were healthy) opened to cope with an ever-increasing import of foreign livestock that was to rank Newcastle as the second-largest port in the UK for this activity.

29 Swirle

Originally the name of a stream that rose near Shieldfield and which initially formed Newcastle's eastern boundary before being culverted to form a short street. Now flanked by modern office buildings, it also has two public works of art nearby, the Swirle Pavilion and Half Moon stone sculpture.

30 The Battlefield and Brickfield

No known military conflict was ever fought here and the name probably has more to do with gambling on the outcome of either dog or cockfights. The clay in this part of Tyneside was ideal for making bricks, for which there was a huge demand, but generally unsuitable for use in local potteries.

11 Gateshead – Pipewellgate to the Goat Inn

1 Pipewellgate

Of 13th century origin, this street was initially 'the abode of some ancient and wealthy families' until it became overcrowded with poorly built tenements and noxious trades at the foot of, and along a damp hillside. The area is now landscaped. Pipewellgate was about 300 yards long and no more than three yards wide. Scavengers sold the 'disgusting refuse' as manure. In 1843 the area had the second highest mortality rate in the UK with only three privies to cope with a population of 2,040. The name Pipewellgate is thought to refer to 'the [wooden] pipes or conduits [to carry water] terminating in an adjoining field'.

2 Iron Foundry, Pipewellgate

Among its varied output was the world's third steam locomotive (illustrated). It was built in 1805 for its designer, Richard Trevithick, and was the first in the North East. It proved too heavy for its wooden rails and never left the works, but it influenced later designs by the Stephensons. An oil business now more than covers this riverside site.

Gateshead Libraries & Arts

Pipewellgate, 1886.

2

6

1

3

4

Bridge Street

7

5

11

Queen's Head Yard

Sun Yard

9

8 Bottle Bank

10

Half Moon Lane

High Street

A view from the river, 1886. The arrow marks the Fountain Inn. It stretched from the street down to the river with steps to the water.

3 Fountain Inn, Pipewellgate

One of five pubs in the street, it had previously been a residence in which George Fox, the founder of the Society of Friends, had met his Quaker followers on a visit to Gateshead in 1657. A modern building on the site now houses a night club.

4 Police Station, Pipewellgate

A new police station opened here in 1845 as an improvement on a lock-up in Bridge Street where one prisoner had managed to escape by knocking down a wall. It closed in 1868 when a new Police Station opened in Swinburne Street. The large windows on the ground floor seem to suggest a shop. Eventually the River Police occupied the building (rebuilt in 1910) until it became a restaurant.

5 Tenements, alleys and yards around Half Moon Lane

Crowded with tenements, narrow alleys, courts and yards, there was also a variety of industry here, including a glass bottle factory, Greene's tannery, two builders' yards, five clay pipe factories and several blacksmiths. A modern hotel and apartments now dominate the area.

6 Timber Yard

Tanneries were often situated near to timber yards, as in this case, because of the ready supply of bark needed for the tanning process. A modern hotel now covers the yard.

7 Bridge Street

A medieval thoroughfare, virtually demolished in preparation for the new Tyne Bridge in the 1920s, now landscaped.

8 Bottle Bank

One of the earliest inhabited parts of Gateshead and the only approach, though steep and dangerous, to the river crossing until Church Street was formed as a bypass in 1790. Crowded with tenements, shops and pubs, it was largely demolished in

The Queens' Head Hotel, High Street, advertises in 1866.

University of Newcastle upon Tyne

A detail from J.W. Carmichael's painting of the High Level Bridge, c.1849. The police station is central. Pipewellgate is on the left.

the 1920s in preparation for the new Tyne Bridge. It is thought Bottle is derived from 'Botl' which was Anglo-Saxon for a dwelling or some other form of habitation.

9 Goat Inn, Bottle Bank

A pub 'where a person could get drunk, commit an offence, and be arrested, tried and sentenced without leaving the building', because it had other rooms which were used as a police station and a court. The goat's head visible at the corner of the building is a reminder of the possible origin of Gateshead's name 'where goats once grazed on the headland'. The Tyne Bridge abutments now cover the site. The Goat Inn sign can be seen in the Shipley Art Gallery.

10 Half Moon Lane

Originally known as Bailey (or Bailiff) Chare, it was re-named in the 18th century after the Half Moon Inn on the corner of Bottle Bank. Whilst the street has survived as Half Moon Lane, the pub has been replaced by modern apartments.

11 The Queen's Head Hotel, High Street

One of seven inns on High Street operating as carriers.

1 St Mary's Parish Church

Little of the early medieval church remains intact after severe damage during the Civil War (1640s), the Great Fire of 1854 and in two more recent major fires (1979 and 1983). The church has been deconsecrated and the congregation moved to St Edmund's Church in High Street. Phillips the Auctioneers occupied the building for a few years. It will re-open as a heritage centre for Gateshead in 2008.

2 St Mary's Anchorage, St Mary's Churchyard

In 1340 the Bishop of Durham sanctioned the construction of the original anchorage within which to lock up an Anchoress (a religious hermit) for the remainder of her life. The building became Gateshead's only school during the 17th century and remained so for the next 150 years. In 1834 over 100 boys and girls were receiving a full syllabus education including Latin and Greek at a cost of a guinea per quarter, French was half a guinea per quarter extra. The original anchorage building attached to the church was destroyed during the Great Fire of 1854 and replaced with another structure (now demolished) to enable the school to continue. The school closed in 1878 because it could not attract a head master at the going rate of £12 a year. Various organisations, including the Town Council, also used the building as a venue for their meetings.

3 The Trollope Mausoleum, St Mary's Churchyard

Legend has it that this mausoleum was built by Robert Trollope, architect of Newcastle's Guildhall in the 1650s, for his own use (he died 1686) with the following epitaph:

Here lies Robert Trollope,
Who made yon stones roll up, [Newcastle's Guildhall]
When death took his soul up,
His body filled this hole up.

Substantially rebuilt 200 years later without any reference to the Trollopes, it now contains the burial vault, with inscriptions relating to the Greene family who had by this time intermarried with the Trollopes. John Greene & Sons were wine merchants and tallow chandlers in Gateshead. Thomas Hedley, the Newcastle soap manufacturer, initially worked for them as a junior clerk (see page 81).

4 Cannon Street

Formerly known as 'High Church Chare', its present name may refer to the ecclesiastical term 'canon' which is sometimes used to describe a parish priest. A map of 1827 identifies the thoroughfare as Canon Street.

5 Oakwellgate

Regarded as 'the fashionable quarter of Gateshead' in 1811 and described a few years later as 'wide and airy' it is said to be named after 'an ancient well once overshadowed by a broad branching oak'.

6 Bush Inn, Oakwellgate

This imposing former three-storey dwelling house with a central pediment over a carriageway entrance served as Gateshead Council Chamber and Police Station from 1836 to 1844. Demolished in 1955, various commercial businesses now operate on this site.

1

10

9　Church Walk

2

3

7　Church St

8

Church St

4　Cannon St

6

5　Oakwellgate

7 Church Street

Designed by the prominent Newcastle architect, David Stephenson, it opened in 1790 as a bypass for the congested Bottle Bank. Again, preparations for the new Tyne Bridge in the 1920s were responsible for much of its disappearance.

8 Dwellings between Church Street and Bottle Bank

This area of densely packed dwellings was also cleared in preparation for the new Tyne Bridge which opened in 1928.

9 Church Walk

Part of this street was destroyed as a result of the Great Fire of 1854.

10 Aftermath of the Great Fire of 1854

This vacant area near the river and to the west of, and below, St Mary's Parish Church resulted from the disastrous fire that seriously affected both sides of the river. At least 800 families needed financial assistance and a minimum of 53 people lost their lives, including Alexander Dobson the 26-year-old son of architect John Dobson. The devastated area is now largely covered by the abutments and towers of the Tyne Bridge which opened in 1928.

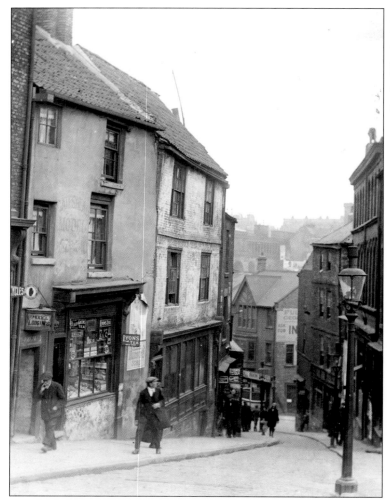

Bottle Bank in 1925. It's hard to believe that this was the main route down to the river crossing until 1790. After that date Church Street improved the situation. These old buildings would soon disappear in preparation for the new Tyne Bridge.

Left, the devastation after the 1854 fire.

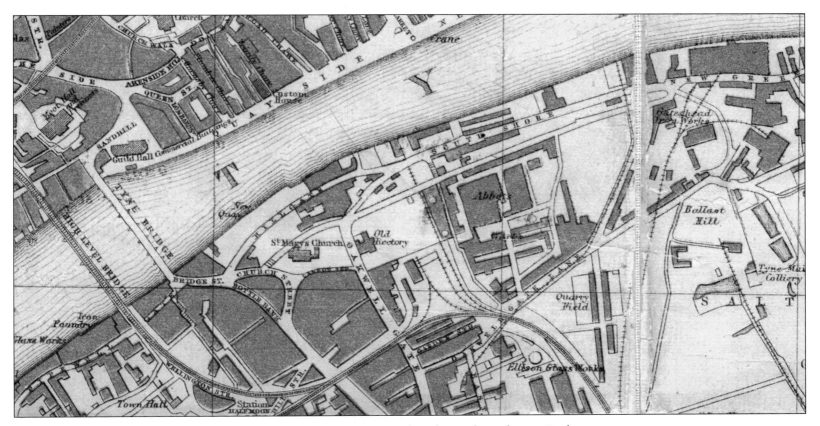

Christie's map of 1865 (enlarged) shows Gateshead from the High Level Bridge to the Park Iron Works.

13 Gateshead – Oakwellgate to the Park Iron Works

To the east of the Rector's field lay the remainder (around 400 acres) of the Bishop of Durham's former hunting park which gradually became industrialised with foundries, collieries, roperies, glass works, chemical works and railways.

1 Old Rectory and Gardens, Oakwellgate

Probably dating from the mid 17th century, it replaced the earlier Rectory destroyed during the Civil War. Increasing industrialisation prompted a move in 1839 to a new Rectory at Bensham, while the old Rectory initially served as a Co-op store, then as a library (with 12,000 volumes) for the North Eastern Railway and as an Institute offering science and art classes. More recently it became a Railwaymen's Social Club, at a time when the North Eastern Railway was Gateshead's largest employer. The Brandling Arms pub was added to the front of the old Rectory. The area is now covered by a car park.

2 Public Baths and Wash-houses, Oakwellgate

They opened in 1854 as a scheme by the corporation to clean up 'one of the dirtiest and most unwholesome places in the Kingdom'. The bath cubicles, 18 male and five female, were regarded as expensive and remained little used, a 'first class' bath cost sixpence while twopence paid for a 'second class' bath. On the other hand the laundry facilities were considered well worth the hourly charge of one penny which included use of the 'ingenious' wringing machines. Another car park now covers this site.

3 Gas Works

From the early 1700s it was known that gas could be obtained by the heating of coal, but it was not until decades later that the process became widely used, largely driven by the need to light the increasing number of factories and workshops. Up to this candles (mainly from animal fat) and then oil (either vegetable or whale) had been used, but they gave poor illumination, a foul smell and black smoke. At this time householders were obliged to light the street outside their dwellings with lanterns until midnight and many people only travelled on nights when the moon was full.

The gasholder behind the Rectory, for the storage of coal gas, presumably to meet the ever increasing demand for industrial lighting, dates from around 1850. Gateshead's first gas works appeared at Pipewellgate in 1819 and another early gasholder can be seen in the picture within the Park Iron Works. To make coal gas, the coal was heated in retort ovens. The resulting gas was stored in large circular gasholders until it was piped to factories, homes and streets as required. The gasholders, which rose and fell according to the quantity of gas within, were secured within a metal frame of columns and girders to permit the incorporation of counter weights. A major by-product of the process was coke, which was very much in demand as a smokeless fuel. For street lighting, lamp lighters were employed daily to light and then extinguish individual gas mantles. There are street lights outside the public baths. Coal gas was gradually superseded by electricity and natural gas, which is not stored in gasholders. A car park and part of the Sage Gateshead now cover the former gas works.

4 Rope Works, Haggie Brothers

David Haggie (1782-1851) the founder of a rope making dynasty and the son of a Scottish weaver, began to make fibre ropes here with a partner before 1800. He was also in partnership with his brother-in-law, Peter Hood, in a local timber business. He retired at 60, and the ropery was then carried on by two of his sons and known as Haggie Brothers. Another son, Robert Hood Haggie, had meanwhile moved away to begin his own rope making business at Willington Quay. Haggie's was considered a good employer. An 1843 enquiry revealed that the youngest boy employed was 12 years old, work rarely exceeded ten hours daily for a six day week (work began at 5am in summer and 6.30am in winter), canteen facilities were provided for breakfasts and mid-day dinners and boys' wages varied between three and four shillings a week. In 1845 a gigantic rope was manufactured for the Liverpool and Manchester Railway. It measured three miles in length, had a circumference of eight inches (20cm) and weighed 13 tons. The Gateshead works were taken over by British Ropes in 1924 and closed in 1993. Today the cleared site lies vacant between the Sage Gateshead and the Baltic.

5 The Park Iron Works, John Abbot and Co. Ltd

In 1835 John Abbot, grandson of the founder, moved here to lease about 15 acres of land and begin to manufacture a huge variety of items from engines to nails and tin tacks for a world-wide market. River frontage, and later railway facilities, contributed greatly to the success of the business. The ironwork for Newcastle Central Station train sheds was produced here in around 1848. Employing between 1,500 to 2,000 workers at its peak, the works closed in 1909. Today the Sage Gateshead occupies the site.

6 Flour Mill

Dating from the mid 18th century it was first used as a woollen cloth factory, then a flour mill, then a brewery. The building was finally absorbed into the Park Iron Works.

7 Oakwellgate Railway Station site

Oakwellgate station opened in 1839 as part of the new Brandling Junction Railway. It needed to be built on a massive raised platform supported by an arched retaining wall (still visible) to lift the rail tracks to match the height of the rail bridge over High Street. The railway was designed for freight and passengers and worked by using a mixture of locomotives, horses and rope haulage to connect Redheugh Quay with South Shields and Monkwearmouth. This avoided expensive and often unreliable river transport. Once the position of the future High Level Bridge over the Tyne had been decided, Greenesfield station was built nearby, effectively making Oakwellgate redundant in 1844. An inclined, curved and cobbled road leading from street level up to the Oakwellgate station has been retained as the approach to the Sage Gateshead car park which now covers the site. Railway sidings occupied the area for much of the time since the 1840s.

The Coaly Tyne

The Tyne was a busy river at the time John Storey painted his panorama, with a commercial history that went back a long way, but the wind of change was blowing over the water and years of neglect were at last being put to rights.

Newcastle Corporation had enjoyed a monopoly over the river and its banks since Royal Charters of the 1200s. The Charters were granted partly because the Tyne was seen as a barrier against the threat of the Scots. In later centuries, when challenged on its crippling monopoly, Newcastle would plead 'no town apart from itself should be on the Tyne' resulting in cases such as Shields fishermen having to sell their catch in Newcastle, and all brewing of ale and baking of bread having to take place there too.

A major complaint against Newcastle Corporation was its neglect of the river. It seems that less than half of river tolls collected were used to maintain and improve the waterway. The result was sandbanks, shallows (often caused by ships dumping ballast to avoid tolls), obstructions, no docks, few quays, and no serious dredging. Apparently some of the tolls had been diverted to 'light, pave and scavenge the streets of Newcastle.'

The poor state of the river by the 19th century made ferry journeys (often the only practical mode of transport) unpredictable and not for the faint-hearted. Passengers prepared for the worst with frequent groundings and the occasional need for rope ladders. It was possible at very low tides to 'plodge' across the river between Newcastle and Gateshead.

The only people to benefit from this deplorable state of affairs were the Tyne keelmen who were able to use their strength and skill to operate flat-bottomed barges (keels) taking cargoes (mainly coal) down the river to waiting vessels at Shields.

Newcastle's river monopoly ended in 1850 with the establishment of the Tyne Improvement Commission which was made up of representatives from Newcastle, Gateshead, North Shields, South Shields and the Admiralty. One of the main factors pushing change was that the Tyne was no longer the only coal port on the North East coast and therefore ships unable to navigate the Tyne were beginning to favour Sunderland, Hartlepool or Blyth. Railway development just increased competition for business. Something had to be done.

The river was improved gradually. New docks were established at Howdon and Jarrow; walls were built at Newcastle Quayside; obstructions were removed; river channels were straightened, and substantial dredging took place. By 1870 the Tyne had become the UK's third largest port. An indication of just how much the river had improved can be judged by the time it took for high tide to reach Newcastle bridge, a distance of about ten miles from the estuary. In 1860 the time was one hour, but by 1879 it only took 12 minutes.

In 1863-4 steam ships were leaving Newcastle twice a week for ports such as London, Hull, Leith and Hamburg, together with weekly sailings to Aberdeen, Lynn, Yarmouth and Rotterdam. At the same time sailing traders were

Newcastle upon Tyne, 1836, from a drawing by G. Balmer.

operating less frequently than steam ships to the following destinations: Arbroath, Berwick, Boston, Dundee, Ipswich, Montrose, Scarborough, Stirling/Alloa and Yarmouth.

A major national sport at this time was professional rowing and competitive racing for reasonable sums of money took place on the Tyne usually between the High Level Bridge and Scotswood Bridge, a distance of around four miles. Tens of thousands would line the river for a major event. The Tyne was to produce three world champion rowers between 1845 and 1868 – Harry Clasper, Bob Chambers and James Renforth. It was at Harry Clasper's ceremonial dinner at Balmbra's Music hall in 1862 that Geordie Ridley sang his *Blaydon Races* (horse racing meetings) for the first time.

1 Keel

A keel lowers her mast before 'shooting' through the low arches of the bridge. Another keel can be seen approaching further down river. More keels lie off the Gateshead shore.

2 Trading vessels

Tyne ships traded all over the world. Exports included coal, glass, lead, grindstones, bricks, tiles, iron products, eathernware, chemicals and manufactured goods. Imports included wine, spirits, fruit, tobacco, corn, sugar, flax, hemp, esparto grass (for papermaking), and, importantly, ballast. Ballast included, where possible, products used in industrial processes like limestone, flint, sand, iron bar, timber, potters' clay and hides.

3 Fishing craft

These small sailing boats are lying off the Fish Market.

4 Dutch coasting barge

This old-fashioned vessel has lee boards to enable her to negotiate heavy winds.

5 Steam tug

The steam tug is guiding a 'painted port' brig as she leaves her berth. Having unloaded her cargo the brig is riding high out of the water.

6 Coastal sloop

The sloop is setting her mainsail.

7 Trading brigantine

A brigantine had two masts. Steam would gradually come to displace sail as the years went by. The last engineless long haul sailing ship to be registered on the Tyne was the *Ravenscraig*, sold to Norway in 1901.

8 Ferries

River passenger steam paddle ferries cluster round the landing stage. There were regular services up and down the river. The fare was a few pennies, depending upon where you sat. These ferries belong to the Red Star Line and its rival the Percy Line (as noted by the review of the picture in the *Newcastle Daily Chronicle*, 1862). The Tyne General Ferry Company would be set up in 1862 by Act of Parliament.

9 Steam collier

Behind the collier the hydraulic crane seems to be lifting a boiler either into or out of the ship.

10 Paddle steamer

This is a coastal or short sea crossing passenger carrying steamer.

5   6   7   8   9   10

Some sources

Addyman, J. & B. Fawcett, *The High Level Bridge and Newcastle Central Station*, 1999

Archaeologia Aeliana, 1937, 1969

Ayris, Ian, *A City of Palaces*, Tyne Bridge Publishing, 1997

Ayris Ian & Patricia Sheldon, *On the Waterfront*, Tyne Bridge Publishing, 1995

Bennison, B. & J.P. Merrington, *Centenary History of the Newcastle Breweries*, 1990

Campbell, W.A., *Gas Lighting in Newcastle*, 1985

Faulkner, T. & Andrew Greg, *John Dobson*, Tyne Bridge Publishing, 2001

Fraser, C.M. & K. Elmsley, *Tyneside*, 1973

Glendinning, D., *Thomas Bewick*, Tyne Bridge Publishing, 2003

Guy, Andy, *Steam and Speed*, Tyne Bridge Publishing, 2003

Hall, Marshall, *Artists of Northumbria*, 2005

Lovie, David, *Buildings of Grainger Town*, 1997

Manders, Frank, *Cinemas of Newcastle*, Tyne Bridge Publishing, 1991, 2005

Manders, Frank & R. Potts, *Crossing the Tyne*, Tyne Bridge Publishing, 2001

Manders, Frank, *A History of Gateshead*, 1980

McCarthy, Sean, *The Theatre Royal*, 1988

McCord, Norman, *North-East England*, 1760-1960, 1979

Middlebrook, S., *Newcastle upon Tyne: its Growth and Achievement*, 1950

Moffatt, Frederick C. *History of the Northumbria Police*, 1993

Munden, Alan, *Jesmond Parish Church*, 2006

Pevsner, Nikolaus, *Buildings of England: Northumberland* 2nd edition revised by John Grundy et al, 1992

Redfern, Barry, *Victorian Villains*, Tyne Bridge Publishing, 2006

Redhead, Lynn, *Hospitals*, Tyne Bridge Publishing, 1996

Rennison, R.W., *Water to Tyneside*, 1979

Wells, J.A., *Railways of Northumberland and Newcastle upon Tyne 1828-1998*, 1999

Older books

Boyle, J.R., & W.H. Knowles, *Vestiges of Old Newcastle*, 1890

Collingwood Bruce, J., *Handbook to Newcastle upon Tyne*, 1863

Guthrie, J., *River Tyne*, 1880

Johnson, R.W., *The Making of the Tyne*, 1898

Oliver, Thomas, *A New Picture of Newcastle and Gateshead*, 1831, 1844

Some of the varied advertisements in Newcastle Daily Chronicle during the 1860s.

Index